THE HEART OF CHINA

OF

HOW MINDFULNESS CHANGED MY LIFE

D1067137

Todd Cornell

"The Heart Of China Series," readings for Peacemakers

Cultur668 Publishing

Cultur668 Publishing is a subsidiary of Cultur668 LLC www.HeartOfChinaSeries.com

ISBN: 978-1-7321804-2-0

For my dear friend, Phil. A beautiful man, a wonderful soul, simply searching for meaning and happiness in a complex world.

The Author

For over 20 years, Todd Cornell resided, studied, and worked in Taiwan, Hong Kong and Mainland China. He speaks and reads fluent Mandarin Chinese. During his business career, he worked for multiple global corporations in cross-cultural management positions.

The languages and cultures of China fascinate him. He reads the Dao, Yi Jing - Book of Changes, and other Eastern philosophies and Buddhist texts in Chinese and practices *Anapanasati* meditation based on the teachings of 空海法師 the Venerable Kong Hai, a Taiwanese monk.

Shortly after arriving in Asia, he quickly forgot the stories told to him about those who do not follow a certain belief set as being doomed. For him, this was no longer an option.

The Editor

A woman of many facets, Andrea Lantican has tackled projects in copy editing, poetry, journalism, magazine publication and many areas in the arts and creative design spectrum. She is a lover of the arts and is passionate about philanthropy.

Foreword

Mindfulness has quickly become a buzzword. Today, we use it in a plethora of surroundings to signify elements that fit the context of the conversation. However, mindfulness is a way of life. It is not a word to apply when we could easily use the words, "pay attention" or "be careful." To be mindful depends on paying attention, but the way we do so is not the same as one would assume. It is a more attentive approach to noticing inner experiences if you will. It works in concert with the breath.

The best way to be successful with mindfulness practice is to commit yourself and hold strong. Afterward, connect with friends and family who support you. Surrounding yourself with those who have similar constructive interests and habits is a good way to build up a strong support network during challenges. Join meditation groups and practice daily, even if it is only for five minutes. Don't break the continuum. One of the most important things to do in order to build a successful mindfulness practice, during and outside of meditation, is persistence. Become persistent against the critical inner dialogues and suspicions!

I base a successful mindfulness practice on a grounding in meditation. It is the training field for mindfulness. As we become more adept with the exercise, we learn to prevail with the practice.

During meditation, we first train the mind to focus on the breath and return to the breath with a mental nudge when it wanders. We observe emotions and reactions around a variety of thoughts, memories, and feelings. We notice random thoughts that come from the depths of our minds, surfacing for no apparent reason, but do not represent who we are. By doing this, we realize that memories and feelings are powerless against us as we sit quietly, noticing that the fears do not bring into being that which is feared. We find peace of mind in learning to support a peaceful mind through mindfulness. I invite you to join the many people who, over the ages, have found peace of mind and fullness of heart through a mindfulness practice.

Mindfulness is an intangible tool practiced and applied anytime, anywhere. Wherever you have access to your breath, you have access to mindfulness practice. During stressful communications, difficult relationships, challenges in life, school, or business, mindfulness is a moment of peace. It is a place to find calm amid the fast-paced, skin-deep, superficial challenges with which we constantly must interact. Through mindfulness, we realize that mental distractions are not reality. We only find reality in the breath's moment and the sensations of the body.

Some of this may speak a message. You may already have a certain sense deep in your psyche, or perhaps find it hard to make sense of. Just know that this practice has endured millennia and has been shown to improve lives. It's difficult, but anything of value will be. Developing a mindfulness practice requires dedication and resilience.

Only "I" make it fail. Only "I" make it succeed.

Todd Cornell

Fort Collins, CO September 2021

Suggestions For Reading This Book

This book includes activities in most chapters. To get the best results, I suggest you practice the activities in each chapter for a week before moving on to the next chapter. This way, you will establish a firm foundation for the practice in the next chapter. Otherwise, you can read the book from start to finish and then go back to complete the activities — again, spending a week on each before moving on to the next.

It's important to do the activities, especially if you're new to mindfulness. By becoming comfortable with individual activities over a week, you may experience results faster.

We all have our ideas about life. Many times, habits support these ideas. While reading this book, notice your thoughts or reactions that arise. They may attempt to contradict or derail the concepts and practices introduced. Maintain an open mind, place previous understandings to the side, and consider new perspectives. Be completely honest with yourself and don't jump to habitual conclusions about life. There is much that will never be knowable in our brief life span. However, the lessons left by those who came before us offer insight and a path to finding peace of mind and developing a compassionate heart amid a rat race.

Editor's Pick

The Editor's Pick is the favorite phrase or idea selected by Andrea during the editing process.

Disclaimer

Apply the information offered in this book only when it will not cause harm to yourself or those around you. Never practice meditation while driving or operating mechanical equipment or tools. Consult with a medical professional if you have any doubt about the safety of practicing anything in this book.

A percentage of the purchase from this book is donated to a mindfulness-based non-profit organization.

Thank You

Contents

Acknowledgments

I would like to acknowledge my teacher, 空海法师 the venerable *Kong Hai*. He taught me the profound and life-changing skills of focusing on the breath and experiencing the present moment.

My mother, who always respected my choices, never judged my failures, and always praised my successes.

Becca LaPole for initial editing support as I began writing this book. The organizations that allowed us use their space and the many people who supported my mindfulness groups in California, Wyoming, and Colorado.

And Rascal (2006 - 2019), my West Siberian Laika, who traveled with me from Harbin, China to the US. We learn much about life and love from our four-legged brothers and sisters!

Difficult to detect and very subtle,
The mind seizes whatever it wants;
So let a wise one guard one's mind,
For a guarded mind brings happiness.
—Dhammapada 36

Why Mindfulness?

"If you want to conquer the anxiety of life, live in the moment, live in the breath." — Amit Ray

So, what is mindfulness? This is a question many have perhaps asked and to which most likely not received a definitive response. Everyone basically approaches mindfulness the same, but the experience is not the same. One person's story and experience may not coincide with someone else's.

In the first chapter of Lao Zi's (Lao Tzu), *"Dao De Jing (Tao Te Ching),"* a Chinese philosophical classic that offers insight into the universal truths of nature and existence, it says, "The Dao that can be spoken of is not the universal cycle. The name that can be uttered, describes not the thing named."[1] This precept expresses the idea that the true and real are not easily expressed in words.

Many times, words are confusing but we easily understand direct experience. Experience is tangible. Yet, we are so closely connected to words that we forget that experience is foremost. At times, in more extreme cases, thoughts and words can modify the authentic experience.

---

1   Paraphrased by the author.

When we describe authentic experiences with words, it evokes diverse responses with different individuals as each person has their own interpretation of words brought out by different experiences. In our minds, to maintain our illusions, we may apply wording untrue to the authentic experience in order to modify the memory to be as we wish.

To gain the most in the practice, it is important that we are honest with our thoughts and experiences to keep them as pure as possible. This may require us to look at things in ourselves that we have avoided looking at before.

Mindfulness is a common experience, a shared practice, and yet, experienced individually. Either way, when practiced with resoluteness, the results are the same: increased calm, clarity, compassion, and productivity. These are the positive results of applying mindfulness. They support us with our daily routine, even during mundane tasks.

Mindfulness is an individual expression of skills based on a daily meditation practice, which is founded on an intimate awareness of the breath.

When we focus our attention on the breath, we experience a calm clarity that is not present when we allow the mind to move along on its own volition. Just like Fido, if the mind isn't kept on a leash, it may run off and get us in trouble. The leash is the breath. By maintaining a consistent awareness of the breath, we will notice the subtle activities of the mind and respond by making necessary adjustments that will nudge awareness back to the breath.

Meditation

Words commonly known to correspond with the idea of meditation are concentration, deep thought, introspection, pondering, reflection, rumination, and self-examination. One of the earliest Buddhist forms of mindful meditation, *Anapanasati*, stems from written records dating back to over 2500 years ago. Following the death of the Buddha Gotama, they were kept close by his followers and family members. This is the form of meditation that Gotama practiced to achieve enlightenment and later taught his followers. There are no religious or superstitious qualities about early Buddhist meditation. In fact, it is just the opposite. It is a practice that guides us to base ourselves in reality and loosen the hold of the lesser mind.

Nevertheless, mindfulness is more than meditation. It is a full-fledged awareness based on the skills we nurture through meditation. Just as the Buddha taught, it is a practice based on awareness of the breath, established individually through a relationship with each breath inhale and exhale.

We simply reach an understanding of the in-breath and the out-breath. We feel the sensation of the breath around our nostrils or the tip of our nose. We notice the pauses and the many characteristics that each breath holds. Just like a flower, each breath is an individual worthy of notice and worthy of appreciation. As you read this, reflect on your breath. If you notice some subtleties mentioned above, you have a propensity toward sensitivity and insight. That is a great foundation to move forward into your practice.

We can all improve our relationship with the breath and strengthen our abilities to notice the subtle characteristics of each one. By doing so, we notice improvements in our focus, work quality, and relationships.

Practicing mindfulness offers a time buffer we didn't previously have. Sometimes, it's just a fraction of a second more that affords us the time we need to make better decisions and improve the potential outcome of a situation. Maybe it's just something as small as the acknowledgment of an individual, managing an emotion-filled response, or how we reply to a client during a critical conversation. Transformations happen in a split second and these changes carry an impact on our lives.

So, what do we gain from practicing mindfulness? Mindfulness gives us the ability to break the hold of craving and desire produced in the mind. It gives us the skills to manage distractions caused by the mind, supporting us to focus on what we need to do at the moment. For instance, when working on a project, we may become distracted or unfocused because the mind is weak from possible stress. This causes the mind to become rigid.

Editor's Pick

"When we notice negative and defeating thought processes, we can change destructive thoughts to constructive ones."

Applying Mindfulness

Connect with the breath. Take deep breaths and confirm you are getting the required oxygen to the brain. Next, notice your physical and mental state. By doing this, you express an intention to put your best thoughts forward, even during moments it may not be the first choice of the ego-mind. Expect your mind to always invent excuses for why this practice — a mission to reclaim mental property — may not be such a good idea.

The mind likes to do what's easiest. Routinely, it does nothing, and often, what it's always done — daydream, ruminate, worry. Perhaps, like myself, you direct dramas. The mind wants to protect itself from hurt, pain, and deficiency from what it considers meets its needs and interests. Many times, this includes producing detailed dramas and getting carried away with one-sided narratives. It could be the force of habit of not taking accountability, even when our views and thoughts are incorrect. This challenge alone may be the first challenge we experience when applying mindfulness to our relations, work, and other aspects of our lives.

Because mindfulness is a practice of focusing on the breath during activities, by doing so, we foster a clear train of thought and maintain a consistent line of focus. This is what gives us the flexibility to respond to the inside and outside stimuli in a constructive and relaxed fashion. One reason for this may be that we become more in tune and connected to our experiences. Over time, we perfect the practice of mindfulness through the exercise of meditation. Consequently, it takes time. However, in regards to the time spent establishing mindfulness practice, it is a minimal expense in comparison to the long list of benefits it develops.

Some describe mindfulness as a skill or practice that allows us to revive our authentic person. We achieve this by noticing self-talk and changing the tone of our thoughts. When we notice negative and defeating thought processes, we can change destructive thoughts to constructive ones. By noticing critical and selfish thought habits, we can choose to transform them into responses of acceptance and charity.

As we begin to apply mindfulness, we progressively realize the ability to change the way we show up. We incorporate healthier and more beneficial ways to respond to people and situations.

For me, the reaction was frequently one of frustration or anger because things weren't following as planned. In my head, I had expectations that weren't being met or they did not see my opinion as valid. Once I developed practicing and applying mindfulness skills, I noticed I had a new spectrum of choices that I had not known before. I experienced an extra moment of time to revisit my initial reactions, some of which caused me years of unhappiness and suffering.

Now, I not only control the bursts of anger, but more importantly, they are no longer present. What used to be a huge all-engulfing fire in my whole being withered to just a small flicker in my belly.

Do remember, this didn't happen overnight. It took months and years of continued practice. However, if I had not started, I would not have arrived to know the power of a mindfulness practice. Be diligent and honest with yourself and you *will* value the changes that take place in your life.

We are the result of our thoughts, our life is founded on our thoughts, fashioned by our thoughts. If one speaks or acts of an unskillful thought, pain follows, as the wheel follows the foot of the ox that draws the cart.

We are the result of our thoughts, our life is founded on our thoughts, fashioned by our thoughts. If one speaks or acts of a skillful thought, happiness follows, like a shadow that never departs.

—Dhammapada 1-2

It Starts With The Breath

"You are where you need to be. Just take a deep breath."
— Lana Parrilla

Breathing is something we do from the moment we are born and will continue until the moment we die. We all breathe around 20,000 breaths per day, and with most, happening without awareness or intervention. Breathing is the bodily function that one can hack into and control or leave on autopilot.

The breath is also the one innate object that we have available to return our focus on. It is always with us and is the perfect object to shift our awareness towards finding a sense of grounding.

Although, as infants, we all breathe into our belly or stomach, many people in the West don't breathe correctly. Over the years, most of us grew up breathing into our chest and assumed this is the correct way to breathe. Among other reasons, we had no accessibility to anyone to teach us the proper form. However, this method is not an effective way to get oxygen into our system.

There are many reasons we breathe into our chest and we may relate some to stress and anxiety. I've met many people who, while practicing mindfulness, realize they hold their breath. Yet, when we don't breathe effectively, we won't get sufficient oxygen to the brain, and this may increase our stress and anxiety. Just the thought of someone asking me if I know how to breathe is off-the-wall. I mean, I'm alive and upright, aren't I?

Most people from Eastern cultures know we should breathe into our belly to get the best delivery of oxygen to our brain and our system. Though most of us breathe into our chest, breathing into the belly is, in fact, the correct means of breathing which some refer to as "belly breathing."

When practicing mindfulness, one of the first things we want to do is check our breathing to ensure we are breathing correctly.

If you have taken singing lessons or played a wind instrument, you most likely know what belly breathing feels like. You can tell a chest breather by watching the rise and fall of their chest; the chest will rise when breathing in, fall when breathing out, but the belly will remain still.

If you haven't already, assess whether you are a chest or belly breather. One of the first things we need to do before we practice meditation is to breathe in the most efficient way to get oxygen to our brains. As you breathe, do you notice your chest rising and falling or do you notice your stomach expanding out and contracting back? If your chest is rising and falling, you are breathing into your chest. If your stomach is expanding and contracting, you are a belly breather. Either way, you will surely benefit by making adjustments to your breathing habits. If you are a belly breather, consider paying more attention and breathing even deeper into your belly. If you are a chest breather, let's talk about making the switch.

Chest breathing is shallow breathing. It can increase stress and anxiety. As mentioned earlier, it does not facilitate oxygen to the body to support bodily functions at an optimum level. If you don't breathe into the belly, be patient with yourself and your body as you perfect the skill of this method.

Belly Breathing

Let's go over the basics of belly breathing. Even if you breathe into your belly, I would suggest you read through this section to confirm and become more aware of your breathing style.

First, sit in a comfortable and erect position, close your eyes, and imagine a balloon in your belly. Breathe in and out through your nostrils, filling the balloon in your stomach with air. Observe the feeling as it expands. Breathe in deeply and sense the balloon fill up with air. Now, exhale through either your nostrils or your mouth. Feel the balloon in your belly contract as you empty it of air.

Practice this exercise for a few minutes until you are comfortable with the technique and can apply it easily. Pay attention to your breathing throughout the day as you embrace belly breathing. Eventually, it will become second nature. Until then, you will want to notice your breathing to make sure you are breathing effectively.

If you notice tightening in your stomach muscles or resistance from your body, that is normal. You are trying something new and it needs to adjust. Muscle memory may kick in and try to hinder your belly from expanding. Your mind may also warn you that the stomach should be flat, more fitting with our cultural aesthetic values, a form of cultural conditioning. Steer your awareness away from the conditioned thoughts and maintain attention on your breathing, allowing the belly to expand. Don't concern yourself if it feels like your stomach is protruding out. It is most likely an exaggerated feeling from the newness of the belly breathing. As you become accustomed to the technique, you will breathe naturally into your belly and will no longer feel exaggerated.

If you have difficulty practicing belly breathing, simply lie down on your back, place your hand on your stomach, and breathe naturally. By doing this, you will notice you breathe correctly into your belly. Observe your hand rise and fall with the stomach as you inhale and exhale. While doing this, focus your attention on the feeling and sensation of belly breathing, and consider how to reproduce this form of breathing after you stand up. Follow the breath in and out.

After successfully experiencing belly breathing, stand up and notice the difference as you maintain the same way of breathing. Again, note any hesitation from your stomach or your thoughts and relax your stomach muscles as you breathe out.

Learning to breathe correctly, even if it is only when you are paying attention to your breathing, is an important step to hacking stress, relaxation, and increasing your productivity. If you feel anxious, remember to turn your awareness to your breathing and observe if you are breathing into your chest or stomach. Then, take a few deep breaths into your belly and nourish your brain with oxygen. Take note as the sense of relaxation comes over you.

Belly Breathing Practice

Over the next few days, practice belly breathing wherever you find yourself. Simply stop and notice your breathing. The following are suggestions of where you can apply this practice, but feel free to add places to the list from your personal situations.

- Sitting at your desk
- Walking in the park
- Standing in line
- In a meeting
- Sitting at a traffic light
- When you become anxious
- During a meal
- Reading email or a book
- Watching a movie

The fragrance of a flower travels not against the wind, neither sandal-wood, or Tagara and Mallika flowers; yet the kindness of a good person travels despite the wind; a good individual permeates everyplace.

—Dhammapada 54

True Relaxation

"Relax, Recharge and Reflect. Sometimes it's OK to do nothing."
—Izey Victoria Odiase

Relaxation is a state that must be achieved actively and mentally. It doesn't just happen. Relaxation is a choice. It requires awareness and direct integration of our mind, body, and breath. Without the integration among the three, it will be difficult to achieve true relaxation. For instance, if we are not aware of stress, it affects our overall physical and mental state. Thus, it's important that we become intimately aware of these three — mind, body and breath — if we truly want to experience healthful relaxation.

When we don't have healthy stress hacking practices in place, such as ways to recognize and release stress, our lives may become disoriented by the unresolved stress. Mental stress ignites physical stress, which can lead to physical ailments including heart disease and cancer. The physical stress from these illnesses will then increase mental stress that may increase the propensity to mental illness. Stress is a vicious cycle and this is the very reason we need to instill sensitivities and practices in our lives.

In 2017, the American Psychological Society research data shows the top causes of stress in the United States as:

- Future of our nation—63%

- Money—62%

- Work—61%

- Political climate—57%

- Violence and crime—51%

Many people may not be aware of practices to ease stress and support calm. When this is the case, some turn to healthy activities and exercises such as running, bodybuilding, yoga, cycling, Pilates, and CrossFit. On the other hand, some choose to turn to alcohol, marijuana, cigarettes, and other forms of self-medication to deal with stress.

Obviously, we should make healthy choices, but when stress is affecting work and productivity, we may not take off to the gym to exercise or go to the park for a run. However, we can always find relaxation through a calming practice that slows our heartbeat and breath to relax the muscles. Applying this form of relaxation improves overall attitude and productivity when practiced daily.

Balancing Activity Through Non-Activity

Eastern thought teaches the importance of achieving a balance between opposing non-aggressive energies.

Perhaps you have heard of The Book of Changes, also known as the I Ching, or, more correctly, 易经 the Yi Jing. It is an early Chinese classic full of universal wisdom. They base it on the concepts of change observed in nature by Chinese ancestors—founders of early Chinese culture. In fact, the Yi Jing is foundational to Chinese thought, culture, and worldview. Before they created the Chinese writing system, it was already in existence.

Legend has it that Fu Xi (pr. foo shee), the legendary first Chinese Emperor, was the thinker said to be the founder of Chinese cultural thought. This includes farming practices and the Chinese writing system among others.

Fu Xi meticulously observed the four directions. In doing so, he noted the effects and interactions that took place. Interactions which, maintaining certain conditions, induced change. He also noted the influence of energies that harmonize balanced dualities, such as night and day, cold and hot, moon and sun. This awareness is what we understand as "Yin-Yang."

Yin, the feminine energy, and Yang, the masculine energy, are both the ripples and balancing of differing energies. This is a universal harmony created from non-aggressive opposing energies. They are not in sync with human desires or expectations, therefore, when we adapt to such fluctuations in life, a sense of harmony emerges. We perceive universal wisdom notwithstanding the outcomes.

When we observe and understand how non-aggressive opposing energies interact and achieve balance, we are better able to understand the forces that work for or against us in life. The insight and awareness of these energies are innate and reside in our hearts and minds. We need only to be open to it.

According to the Yi Jing, everything has a non-aggressive, or harmonious, counter. To experience the highest success of activity-based practices, there must also be a counter-balancing practice of non-activity.

In All Things, Change Is the Logical Result

In the expression, "When it reaches a pinnacle, it flips," we hear a core phenomenon of the Yi Jing expressing the idea that one energy, yin or yang, will flip to the other after it reaches its highest climactic level.

This prompts us to regard change as a process of one energy reaching its climax, and subsequently flipping to the contrary energy. I consider this the burnout of one energy giving way to the opposite.

Although a switch in energy may be the desired outcome at times, it may not always be what's expected. When we don't manage energies, they may reach a climactic level and flip to the opposite energy. However, nature imposes balancing mechanisms for when we don't possess the skills or conscious awareness to manage it ourselves. Consider when one becomes consumed by the energy of anger and outrage, the result is exhaustion and the need to rest.

In the expression, "静观其变 In silence, observe the change," we hear the call to learn self-control. Silence is the proper state for learning, observance is the key to understanding, and contentment is the fruit of acceptance. When we see the wisdom of change, we will find contentment. Recognizing this universal wisdom is powerful beyond understanding.

Editor's Pick

"In all things, change is the logical result."

Action and Non-action

Action and non-action also require balance and harmony. Here, action or activity refers to any form of movement or any state that is counter to stillness. Consider walking, running, talking, watching television, even working on a computer. These are all activities as they engage the body and the mind in action or activity.

If you've heard about the traditional Shaolin Kung Fu practice, you most likely know that it is a vigorous practice of balancing action and non-action. They built this traditional practice on the foundation of 禅 — Chan.

Chan is the Chinese form of mindfulness that is based on early Buddhism in China. It was later developed into the popular practice of Zen, infamous in Japan.

In the Eastern tradition, before a person becomes adept at action, they must first perfect the art of non-action. In other words, to excel in activity or motion, we should first perfect the state of stillness and calm. The reasoning behind this is simple, yet profound. Like anything, the state of action creates physical and mental vibration and motion in our being. If physical and mental vibration becomes our normal state of being, then we become less sensitive to the state of vibration and motion beyond the healthy balance. It's like a state of continuous action.

Think about stress for a moment, from whichever perspective it means to you. If your normal state of being is at a certain level of stress, then anything beyond that will be virtually indiscernible. It's like creating a ripple on a lake. If you increase the ripple slightly, it will not be obvious. However, if you create a ripple on the surface of a calm lake, the ripple will be distinctly visible. This is the reason they founded the Shaolin practice on mindfulness in relation to the breath. It allows them to execute movement on the foundation of a calm state, like the surface of a calm lake, which facilitates a stronger force in its movement. Grounded, all movement spawns from a state of calm and mindful clarity. From a state grounded in a calm mind, steady body, and breath—at the moment prior to any action, they execute movement while maintaining the grounding throughout.

The reason I explain this is to express the importance of working in a calm state. When we are aware of our mind, body, and breath, we are in a space that is the foundation of higher focus and increased productivity. Just like the Shaolin monks, always return to the calm space. Remain grounded and aware before, during, and after the movement. What we are striving for is similar to that of Eastern practices, but with adjustments to fit the needs of modern Western society.

Relaxing the Body

In the previous chapter, we learned to practice belly breathing. Belly breathing, or breathing, as we will call it from now on, is a foundational skill in mindfulness and key to achieving true relaxation. It is the foundational aspect of mindfulness. Any time we experience anxiety, nervousness, or other forms of stress, just like the Shaolin monks' action-founded-on-non-action practice, we will return our attention to the breath and proceed from there.

Think of the breath as the space to connect with non-action within your being.

In the beginning, you may need to work harder to relax and remain in this state. It's an awareness that should run in your subconscious at all times. You will notice your tense muscles quickly return to this previous state of non-relaxation due to muscle memory. When you notice your muscles returning to the tensed state, continue to focus on it. Breathe into the tension and release on the exhale to relax. Eventually, your previous state of tense muscle memory will be replaced by relaxed muscles and it becomes your new normal.

As you become more familiar with the relaxation practice, you will achieve a more speedy and effective relaxed state within just a few breaths. You may think, "I'll fall asleep if I get too relaxed," when in fact, this is merely an assumption. Culturally, we tend to relate relaxation with sleep or sluggishness, however, the relaxation we are calling attention to is the physical and mental state that we should maintain even during our active moments. Consider the force of action that the Shaolin practitioners achieve from a relaxed and focused state of mind. This quality of relaxation is not equal to lethargy, but a state of grounded awareness and mental calm.

Let's Practice Relaxation

Sit comfortably in a chair. A desk chair or stool will do. Rest your hands on your legs, palms facing up or down, whichever is most natural. Place your feet flat on the ground, spaced approximately shoulder-width apart. If you're sitting on a chair with a backrest, do not lean your back against it. You want to balance the entire weight of your body's upper torso on your hips. Sit up straight, not stiff. Sitting naturally, you should have a slight natural curve to your backbone. Balance your head comfortably on your neck and move your head in a circular motion. Slowly, make the circles smaller until you find where your head rests balanced on your neck with no forward or backward pull.

Position your eyes downward at a 45-degree angle and close your eyes lightly to block out any visual distractions. Closing your eyes helps to focus attention on your breath. Continue to breathe naturally and focus your attention on the breath. Don't attempt to control your breathing. Just notice it and allow it to happen naturally. Inhale through your nostrils, filling your belly, then pause and exhale deeply through your nostrils or mouth, gently forcing out all the air. Do this three times. Focus on filling the balloon in your belly and observe your stomach as it expands with the in-breath and contracts with the out-breath. Release any tightness or stress with each exhalation and take note of your physical and mental progression to relaxation.

Performing a Body Scan

A body scan is simply what it suggests. We scan our body to detect tightness or discomfort in our muscles and release the stress. As mentioned earlier, when we distinguish tightness and discomfort, we release it with the out-breath. It's important to get into the habit of releasing tightness and physical stress with each exhalation. This way, it will become habitual and can be performed at any given place and time.

When doing a body scan, start from the top of your head and work your way down to your toes. In your mind, scan your body for any tightness or tension. Become aware of the tension and release the tension with the out-breath. This practice will have a powerful influence on your present mental and physical state.

When relaxing certain areas of your body, like your scalp or back, you may question how to relax it. In the case that you're unsure, just imagine what it would be like. Go through the process of imagining the outcome of relaxation. Thinking of how it will feel will eventually lead to true relaxation. Don't worry if you aren't feeling major changes immediately. Just know that there are changes you will notice over time and move on to the next part of your body.

Apply the following steps, beginning from the top of your head.

Relax your scalp, forehead, and ears. While going through the relaxation practice, use your mind to envision the act of relaxation. This will assist you as you become mindfully connected with the various areas of your body.

Relax your face, eyes, nose, cheeks, lips, and jaw. While relaxing the face, there are muscles that are easily relaxed, such as the forehead and cheek muscles. When relaxing the jaw, notice a small gap between the upper and lower teeth.

Relax your neck. Slightly rock your head to the left and right to help relax your neck. Notice the position where your head balances naturally and sits without pressure on your neck.

Relax your shoulders. Lift your shoulders as if to touch your ears. Hold for three seconds and release. Let your shoulders fall naturally. Repeat this three times while relaxing your shoulders with the out-breath.

Relax your arms. Focus attention on both arms. Let your arms hang naturally and shake them slightly. Pause and notice gravity pulling them down towards the earth. Do this for three seconds and relax with the out-breath.

Relax your hands. Focus attention on your hands. Make a fist with each hand, using all your strength to grip them tightly. Hold for three seconds, then release and let them relax naturally.

Relax your chest. Focus attention on your chest area. Imagine releasing tension from your chest muscles and relaxing them. Relax with the out-breath. Notice the relaxation in your chest.

Relax your back. Focus attention on your back. Imagine releasing tension from your back muscles and relaxing them. Relax with the out-breath. Notice the relaxation in your back.

Relax your belly. Focus attention on your belly. Relax your belly and allow the balloon to fill. Notice your breath as your belly fills with air. Relax and exhale slowly. Notice the relaxation in your belly.

Relax your hips. Focus attention on your hips and buttocks. Imagine releasing tension and relaxing your hips and buttocks. Notice the relaxation.

Relax your upper legs. Focus attention on your upper legs. Imagine releasing tension in your upper leg muscles and relaxing them. Take note of how the muscle relaxation feels.

Relax your calves. Focus attention on your calves. Imagine releasing tension from your calf muscles and relaxing them. Notice the relaxation in your calves.

Relax your feet. Focus attention on your feet. Rotate your feet at the ankles and imagine releasing tension in your foot muscles to relax them. Wiggle your toes. Notice your relaxed feet.

Make It Your Own

This is a basic body scan and a good place to start. As you become more practiced and familiar with each exercise, you will discover other areas to focus on. Feel free to add or remove areas as you see fit to your personal needs.

Once you are well-practiced, you can conduct a body scan as you please. Just like belly breathing, you can practice body scans anywhere and at any time. You will progress as you continue to observe tightness, focus, and relax with the out-breath.

Quick reference list for body scan:

- Head – scalp, forehead, ears
- Face – eyes, nose, cheeks, lips, jaw
- Neck
- Shoulders
- Arms
- Hands
- Chest
- Back

- Belly
- Hips
- Legs – upper leg, calves
- Feet

*The wise who control the body, who control the
tongue, who control the mind, are truly exceptional.
— Dhammapada 234*

Watching The Breath

"Truth is not something outside to be discovered, it is something inside to be realized." — Osho

After practicing belly breathing, we have a basic understanding of how to focus on the breath, along with a beneficial way to breathe from now on. The breath is our point of return when we remember the need to ground ourselves, refocus, or silence our thoughts. Focusing on the breath is key. Wherever you are and whatever you are doing, center your attention on the in-breath and release any tension you notice with the out-breath. It's that simple.

When we breathe into the stomach, we are breathing into the core of our being. The Chinese call it 丹田, *dantian*. The dantian is located three finger-widths below the belly button. They consider this to be an energy center, sometimes referred to as a heating stove in the belly. It is part of the invisible circuitry and network of pressure points existing in our body and models that of an energy network. The energy points, or meridians, create an energy system within our bodies.

The dantian is an important focal point for energy practices such as Tai Chi and Qigong. It's also an important concept in traditional Chinese medicine.

You can breathe into the dantian or breathe into the belly. It's essentially the same. You are breathing in a way that is most beneficial to increase productivity as you are focusing your mind and feeding your brain with oxygen.

By using the breath as the focal point in this practice, you train the mind to focus where you want it to, rather than allowing it the freedom to jump from one task to the next, challenging your productivity and creativity.

In this chapter, we will learn to combine breathing with counting. We do this to train the mind to focus when distracted or under stress. The practice will be the foundation for building the skills and establishing the tools that will support us in improving mood, patience, productivity, and overall efficiency. With persistence and dedicated practice, we will gain these attributes in our increased focus.

Editor's Pick

"Don't let the mind engage you in negative dialogue."

The Breath Cycle

For more convenience, we will use the term "breath cycle" in reference to the breath and its tracking.

A breath cycle is a unit in the practice measuring for clarity. It makes the breath easier to follow and monitor. By understanding it as a single-unit cyclical pattern, we are less apt to the confusion of the individual in-breath and out-breath. Consider the yin-yang symbol and think of the breath cycle in the same way. It is one unit made up of two interconnected parts.

In Eastern thought, we frequently see the influence of *yin-yang*, a concept of two opposing, but not adverse, forces that make up a whole. When I mention, "not adverse," it is not to say they do not incur adversity. However, adversity is not a product of the two forces themselves rather, we perceive it through our cultural interpretations.

Consider the similarity of the yin-yang with the breath cycle. Yin-yang is one "yin" and one "yang", and the breath cycle is one in-breath and one out-breath. They are both complete or made whole by the other.

A breath cycle is one in-breath and one out-breath. That's it. In-breath, out-breath. A breath cycle always ends on the exhalation where we release all tension or stress. Just as we release on the out-breath, we also count on the out-breath.

The Breath Cycle

In-breath   Out-breath (relax)

Take a few minutes to familiarize yourself with the breath cycle. Count each breath cycle in your mind from one to ten, just like the following:

As you breathe in, count "one," breathe out, count "one;" breathe in, count "two," breathe out, count "two;" breathe in, count "three," breathe out, count "three." Continue until the tenth count and repeat.

This practice will help you better grasp the idea of a breath cycle and prepare you for the next part of the practice—counting the breath cycles.

When things pile up on our "To Do" list, we may have a hard time keeping our attention on the tasks at hand, especially those of us who have several things going on simultaneously but are not naturally skilled at multitasking. Thus, we need to build up our concentration and strengthen our attention span. To do this, we focus our attention on counting the breaths. This will train both the person and the mind. Although this may sound strange, you will quickly realize there are many truths to the concept.

After a few weeks of practicing the count of breath cycles, most people sense a separation or a distance from the mind. The mind no longer takes center stage. This is an amazing and enlightening experience when realized. We begin to comprehend that the mind is just an organ like the rest, thus the expression, "You are not your thoughts." A concept that is truly liberating!

Preparing to Sit

Now that you are familiar with the breath cycle and the count of each, you are ready to transform those simple tasks into a powerful practice to change your life. This is a practice you want to commit to daily. Yes, you can do it! Maintain and sustain your good intention. If your head is spinning at the thought of adding one more task to your daily grind, slow down the spinning by completing a ten-count breath cycle to regain focus.

Next, what you want to do is set a time to practice daily. Start with five minutes, perhaps. Consider which part of the day is best suited for you. I would suggest mornings as this is when you are more likely to be refreshed and able to get up five minutes earlier to sit and practice. If you choose the evening, be sure you have the energy following a long day. With that in mind, evenings can be difficult, especially when you are new to meditation practice. When you close your eyes, you may be prone to dozing off. If you do, don't get frustrated worrying about it. Eventually, the mind will figure out what you are doing and stay focused on counting.

You also want to find a space in your home that is quiet. Of course, we can't remove ourselves completely from ambient noise, but finding a place that's as quiet as possible would be best. It's also a good idea to sit in a place where you feel comfortable, a place you can establish as your go-to spot for mindful practice and sitting.

After you have decided where to establish your space, you can decide if you will sit on a chair or a cushion. If you prefer a chair, be sure to use a standard chair with a sturdy seat, like a dining room chair or even a stool, since we will not be leaning on the backrest. Refer to the **Let's Practice Relaxation** section of the previous chapter to review the best practices for sitting on a chair.

Using a meditation cushion or a chair are the best choices, however, it comes down to preference. Sitting on a meditation cushion is my preference as this is how I received my training in Taiwan. If you sit comfortably on a cushion, you may sit in a lotus or half-lotus position, which may be cumbersome for many. If that's you, then you may wish to try Burmese-style, which I learned from a Buddhist Nun in Taiwan who noticed me struggling with the lotus positions.

Burmese-Style Sitting

Sit with your buttocks toward the front of the cushion. Bring your right heel into the crux of your groin. Then, bring the left foot up just outside the right foot. They should both be flat on the ground, one in front of the other with a slight distance between them.

The feet should not be on top of each other, rather one in front of the other; right foot closest to your body and left on the outside the right. Technically, when sitting on a cushion, you want to have a tripod — three points touching the ground: (1) buttocks, and

(2) both knees. This helps to maintain a stable posture to avoid swaying and distracting the mind.

The following directions are the same for sitting on either a cushion or a chair.

Relax your hands and place them comfortably on your legs or knees. Place them facing up or down, whichever is natural for you. Keep them relaxed. I don't recommend practicing a hand gesture or Mudra while doing this form of mindfulness meditation because it requires engaging the mind. Keep action at a minimum to establish a state of non-action allowing the mind to focus on counting the breath cycles.

Check your posture. Maintain a comfortably straight back, not forced or stiff. Be aware of the natural curvature of the spine and don't slouch. Roll your shoulders back slightly to support proper posture. Adjust and balance your head comfortably on your neck by making tiny circular motions until you find the center of gravity. Gravity should also support your upper torso. For the head, find the centering of your upper torso by moving in mini circular rotations, drawing slowly to a stop in the center of balance. Once you have found the right balance of comfort and posture, sit quietly for a moment and notice how it feels.

Check-in with your chin. Your chin should sit lower, slightly tucked down and inward toward your sternum, but not forced. You may sense the back of your head moving up slightly, with a minor pull on the back of your neck as you do this. Maintain a natural relaxed feeling and don't force any adjustments. To reiterate, all the adjusting we do is very minimal and may even seem like there were no changes. That's alright. You will slowly become sensitized to these slight movements and adjustments as you continue your practice.

For each adjustment, sit for three breath cycles to notice how it feels. This way, you can make a mental note for the next time. Doing this will eventually make it easier to sit down and find the right posture with little effort.

To support your sitting posture, you can imagine a string connecting you with the earth below and the sky above. The string runs in from your seat, through your body, and out through the top of your head, connecting you to the earth and sky. You notice a slight tug at the string from the sky. The string pulls slightly upward. As it is being pulled upward, you sense it pulling your body upward. With this, you can put the final touches on your sitting posture.

As you sit and count your breath cycles, return to the string periodically to check your posture and avoid slouching. Slouching is not good for our bodies or minds. If you have poor posture from long hours in front of a computer or just sitting improperly, you may notice soreness after sitting for a while. Without force, maintain good posture and take note of how it feels, but don't label it as good or bad. Bring your attention back to the breath. After continued practice, you will establish new muscle memory that will become the norm. Be sure to consult with your physician if you have back problems or any other challenges for sitting on a cushion. If discomfort persists, you may also consider sitting in a chair, as described earlier.

Basic Meditation—Sitting with the Breath

Now that you have decided where you will sit, what you will sit on, and have established good posture for a meditation experience, we're ready to introduce focusing on breath cycles.

Let's keep it easy at first. For your first week of meditation, schedule five minutes daily. Otherwise, unless you are already meditating for over five minutes, the mind may drive you nuts. Not that it won't, anyway. You'll suddenly remember everything you forgot to do, such as locking your car or sending that email. You will have a plethora of "things" come to mind that will cause a struggle between your intention to settle down and all the distractions the mind will throw your way. Do your best to sit through it and let the thoughts move on. Tell your mind these things can wait five minutes until you're finished.

In this chapter, we learned to count the breath cycles in the section, "Breath Cycles". If you need to review, feel free to refer back to that section. It is at this point that we combine counting breath cycles together with sitting. We call this meditation.

The first thing to do is get settled in your sitting posture. Don't forget to set your meditation timer for five minutes. Afterwards, take three deep breaths into the belly, or dantian. Remember to release tight muscles or tension on the out-breath. Sitting quietly still, look down at a 45-degree angle without moving your head, close your eyes, and focus on your breath. Count your breath cycles—one to ten, just as we did earlier. Complete as many ten-count breath cycles within the five-minute span and do this every day over the next week. When thoughts arise, return your attention to the breath and continue counting.

If you lose your count, start over. Don't even think about it, just go back to one and start again. Don't let the mind engage you in negative dialogue.

Don't expect perfection. It never comes. Be patient with yourself and give yourself space—just five minutes a day over the next week. If you feel you didn't do as well as you should, don't worry. Instead, be proud of your progress.

Truly, wisdom is born of meditation; without meditation wisdom is lost. Knowing this twofold path of gain and loss, one should conduct oneself so that wisdom may increase.
— Dhammapada verse 282

Focus Is More Than Focusing

"Mindfulness should be likened to eating, sleeping, and breathing; not vacation, time away, or play."–Todd Cornell

This is where the skills of mindfulness hit the road! You know those times when you're in a conversation where three people are talking at the same time? Or when you're late for an important meeting and traffic is moving at a snail's pace? That feeling of being stuck with nowhere to turn. The inner feeling of pressure and the mind feels like it might blow. Times when the mind floods your awareness with scenarios — the good and the bad, the excitement and the fear. Stress kicks in and the mind is Johnny-on-the-spot with mostly useless commentary.

When we talk about focus, we refer to inward awareness or noticing. It is through noticing things vying for our attention that we establish focus. The things vying for our attention may be our immediate environment or thoughts in our heads. To achieve focus, we must first enter our awareness. Focus is an internal experience. No one can focus "for" you or know the degree of your capability. However, someone who has built up the skill to focus can look at another person who has not and recognize their struggle.

The Venerable Kong Hai, my mindfulness teacher, says, "Anyone who has experienced higher levels of consciousness can see the same in others who have also achieved them." However, someone who has not achieved these levels of consciousness cannot see them in someone who has. Grounding is much the same with focus. When the stress hits the fan, we need to pull ourselves together and get grounded. Just like focus, grounding is also based on awareness and begins within.

Get Grounded

Getting grounded should not be something we do only when we need grounding. It should be a consistent habitual practice relying on each moment of every day. If we only practice groundedness when we *need* to be grounded, we put undue pressure on ourselves, which adds to the stress. It's like trying to put out a fire with a fan. A fire starts unexpectedly, so you pull out a fan from your back pocket and frantically fan out the fire. Unfortunately, your noble acts fail because you weren't ready. The fire needed more effort than a fan to extinguish. Were you better prepared with a bucket of water, you could have avoided the engulfing of flames. Being grounded is our bucket of water.

When we maintain a grounded state of mind, we need not deal with negative outcomes from stress as it occupies the walls of our minds and into our lives. Much like the Shaolin practitioners who act from a soft place of a calm mind and grounded body (non-action), they are mentally and physically grounded prior to the onslaught of the kicks and punches—stress. It is only in this way that they respond in time to the hard attacks and aggression, otherwise, they will fight a losing battle. The person with the strongest focus may win against the person with brute strength, even at a higher skill level. This is the power of being grounded. It also fits within the Daoist concept of soft versus hard. Hard always succumbs to soft.

So, how do we ground ourselves? We discussed focus, awareness, and grounding. We can also include the word "attention," like in, "to pay attention." This is where words make communicating difficult. These words carry similar meanings but with slight differences in nuance. Now, how do we understand them for appropriate use towards getting grounded?

If we look at the words in more depth using backward design—a practice where we start from the desired outcome and work backward, we discover the best route to achieving desired results.

In this case, our desired outcome is to be grounded. When we ground ourselves, we are ready for what life slings at us, even when we're not expecting it. When prepared, we're able to respond in constructive ways.

Consider this. To be grounded, we also need to be focused, and we base our focus on awareness. To apply focus to the object of awareness, we must be *cognizant*.

In this way, to be focused, we need to be **aware**—awareness based on **paying attention**. (See Figure 5.1) Paying attention may be the most rudimentary skill we're looking at in the practice of achieving groundedness.

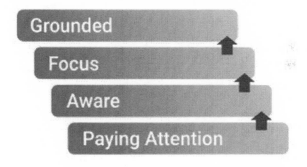

Figure 5.1

With this in mind, the most basic skill for being grounded is to *pay attention*. How many times in our lives have we heard someone say, "Pay attention!"? Perhaps to where it seems trite. However, if we aren't paying attention, we cannot be aware. If we aren't aware, we can't focus. If we aren't focused, we aren't grounded.

The question now is, "What do we want to pay attention to?" Honestly? Everything. Pay attention to everything happening in the present moment. For example, during the breath you're taking at this very moment.

We want to pay attention to our breath. Paying attention to the breath is a core skill for getting grounded. What does this mean? It means to focus on the breath, always.

Of course, rarely do we do so. However, we should always try to. Don't listen to what the mind tells you. It comes up with many reasons not to focus on the breath and why it's a waste of time. Yet, focusing on the breath is as simple as noticing the breath. Notice the breath, then focus on the breath. This is how to ground yourself in the breath. That alone will be one of the most powerful and life-changing steps you do to ground yourself. This awareness prepares your mind like a Shaolin practitioner prepared to support you as you tackle whatever comes your way.

When you have a lot on your plate, focus on what you are doing with your breath at that very moment. This will make your breath the focal point, not the task.

The mind is a tool. Apply the mind to pay attention, notice, be aware, focus, and ground yourself in the breath. The mind is the only tool with which we can accomplish this. However, when the mind is not well managed, it presents challenges to focusing. It randomly tosses around ideas and thoughts from left-field or brings up tasks and things it wants you to do, almost like it pushes back at your attempts to reclaim your mental property.

Interestingly, in the beginning, when one wants to focus and take control, the mind seems to counter the efforts. It's important to be vigilant and resolute in your decisions. It's imperative to not feed the thoughts but stick with what is happening at the moment of this breath. Otherwise, things can get difficult when we slip into engaging the mind's chatter. Rather, notice the chatter and focus your attention on the breath, removing your attentiveness to the chatter. Over time, this will send the message to the mind that you are not listening and the chatter will subside. Silence will prevail over chatter!

Head Chatter

In the previous chapter, we practiced ten-count breath cycles while sitting quietly for five minutes. It's important to complete each full week of activity practice before moving on to the next. If you haven't completed a continuous week yet, please do so before moving on to the activity in this chapter.

If you're ready, add two minutes to the five minutes you practiced last week, increasing your daily sitting to seven minutes this week. Nothing else changes. Simply continue to focus your attention on counting breath cycles and add two minutes.

What did you notice over the past week?

Did you notice thoughts arising while you were meditating? Things that suddenly became pressing? Or how about thoughts similar to, "What are you doing sitting here? You have things to do!"

It is interesting that the mind becomes quite active when we want to sit down and be quiet. When this happens, we should make adjustments by noticing the thoughts and immediately turn our focus to the breath, counting the breath cycles from one to ten.

The mind is constantly active and thoughts frequently arise, but we need not get drawn into the thoughts. This is the importance of focus. When we focus on the breath cycles by paying attention, we notice where our focus lies. When aware of the breath and counting the breath cycles, it supports the mind and keeps it busy, similar to giving a cat a play toy. The toy replaces whatever the cat was paying attention to.

The human mind is much the same. If we aren't paying attention, the mind will hijack at any moment, causing us to count beyond ten or easily forget what number we are on. What do we do when this happens? Some may engage in self-defeating dialogue. If this is you, don't. Return to one and continue counting the breath cycles for seven minutes disregarding the desire to point fingers.

Mental Boot Camp

What are we doing this for? It's a boot camp for the mind. We are training our mind to: 1) Do what we want it to do, and 2) Become focused and grounded. The skills you gain from practicing to focus and count your breath cycles will train your mind to stay focused while you are busy and dealing with stressful situations. We are building the skills to pull our minds away from the thoughts, worries, fears, and scenarios that most of us are familiar with.

For the next seven days, continue sitting and counting the breath cycles. By doing this, you will hone important skills to notice what your mind is doing. Notice when it is wandering and bring it back to the breath.

Practicing Focus

Over the next seven days, and thereafter, apply mindfulness to notice the quality of focus you experience in your daily activities such as the following:

- When someone is talking
- Walking down the street
- Standing in line
- Working on a task
- Reading a book or magazine
- Writing a paper or email
- With friends and family
- Observing your environment

Those whose mind is grounded in the aspects of awareness, without clinging to anything, they experience freedom from attachment clinging to nothing, desires under control, they are full of light and free from suffering.

— Dhammapada 89

Mindful Productivity

"You don't have to control your thoughts. You just have to stop letting them control you."–Dan Millman

In chapter five, we discussed how to get grounded. We looked at the example of an ungrounded Shaolin practitioner during a fight and the most likely outcome.

Consider the mental dialogue of the Shaolin practitioner below who is getting pulled into self-talk due to the lack of practice to focus and grounding.

"Man, I'm hungry. I forgot to buy protein bars."
"Wow, that guy's big. I don't feel like doing this."

Getting caught up with the random thoughts the mind belches, triggered by the environment, memories, feelings, and other stimuli, can be detrimental to our stability and overall effectiveness. These thoughts become distractions which are the reasons causing us to get stressed and lose sight of the task at hand. This is in the space where paying attention is so vital to a successful mindfulness practice. A practice that supports awareness, emotional stability and calm.

If the practitioner grounds themself with the breath and focuses the mind, they would notice the random thoughts. By not engaging them, the practitioner immediately discerns the thoughts as skillful or not skillful. In doing this, within just a fraction of a second, they would know if the thoughts merit engagement or pose a potential danger in doing so.

Maintaining awareness, they notice the random thoughts and return attention to the breath. By returning attention to the breath, they maintain a continued state of focus and grounding. This is the space we want to be in at all times. When one maintains this space in the present moment, it fosters a connection to life and insight beyond understanding. This is something that one cannot achieve from pills or substances.

Now that we have a basic understanding of how the mind and random thoughts need to be managed, we understand how easy it is to get off track on just a simple thought. We learn the importance of keeping a focus on the breath's moment to maintain grounding.

Earlier, we discussed becoming grounded by applying the concept of backward design. Now, we take that one step further and apply the same concept to achieve a state of calm.

Calm is vital for strengthening the power of our minds. As we continue to train the mind in counting the breath cycles, we become more sensitive to subtle details and characteristics we had not noticed before including feelings, thoughts, and emotions.

It's uncanny how the practice of mindfulness somehow opens up an extra millisecond for us to work with. Perhaps it's because we learn to disregard the random thoughts plaguing our minds and realize the problematic thought process and underlying beliefs that clog our thinking.

So, mindfulness affords us extra time to react and opens a myriad of possibilities. With additional time, even an extra millisecond, we are given a moment to think through and make a better choice.

By choosing the thoughts we engage, we avoid unconstructive reactions that may have a controlling grip on us without our knowledge. For instance, in stressful situations where we could avoid reacting unconstructively if we have the sensitivity to disengage the destructive thoughts.

Since mindfulness affords us a moment, we cannot do without it. Calm is an important state to cultivate for a correct response rooted in a place of groundedness.

Thus, a calm mind buys us a fraction of time that we don't otherwise have without it.

Editor's Pick

Many times, these self-defeating thoughts are not evident at the surface of our conscious minds. They become more distinct as we reach deeper levels of awareness through the practice.

The Role of Calm

We strive to maintain a calm and relaxed state at all times. When we are calm, it is easier to notice thoughts and emotions happening in our lives. We are more proficient in regarding them as skillful or not skillful and respond accordingly. We may achieve this by noticing the thought and returning attention to the breath. Perhaps, if it is a destructive and unskillful thought, change it to a positive one. For example, when you notice your mind with the self-defeating thought, "I can't do this," change it to, "I can do this." Afterwards, return focus to the breath.

Many times, these self-defeating thoughts are not evident at the surface of our conscious minds. They become more distinct as we reach deeper levels of awareness through the practice. Sometimes, self-defeating thoughts can be evasive and fleeting, therefore, internal awareness is important to gain insight into our thought process and underlying beliefs.

To be calm we need to be **quiet** and quiet is based on being grounded. (See Figure 6.1) When we are grounded we allow the mind to be quiet by not engaging thoughts that are continually pushed out. Again, thoughts come from surroundings, situations, feelings, smells, sounds, and words that trigger ideas and memories. Of course, sometimes they are useful, but the challenge is to discern them as skillful or unskillful.

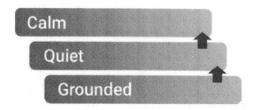

Figure 6.1

To reiterate, calmness requires the need to be quiet which is based on being grounded. Once we have attained a state of groundedness, we can focus on being quiet, essentially dismissing each thought that strikes and instead, focusing on the breath. Some people verbalize everything that comes to mind which is not skillful.

By listening, we show more interest in what others are saying. When we apply this skill, we notice an enormous difference when our mind is yapping causing us to struggle hearing through all the chatter. You can see it in a person's eyes when they are experiencing this state of mental chaos. Eye contact is weak, making it apparent they aren't hearing all that is being said. This is not a characteristic of good interpersonal skills.

By training our minds to be quiet, we cultivate a state of calm. The outward quiet nurtures inward calm. It is through this inward calm, based on the outward expression of quiet, that we maintain groundedness.

In calm, we develop a unique connection to our inner experience — activities in our minds and bodies. We observe reactions and responses, noticing feelings and emotions as they rise and fall. In this state, we gain a clear and profound awareness, all while choosing the best ways to respond. A perfect world scenario, you may think. True, and nothing of value comes without work. This thought applies well to mindfulness. It's difficult, but the results are invaluable.

Alternative to readjusting every time the mind shines floodlights on a sensation or scratching every mental/physical itch that appears, we should continue to practice meditation and sitting still. With this, we notice what is happening and become aware of thoughts and feelings as we focus on the breath. It's in doing this we experience groundedness.

Once grounded, we continue to apply the skills of paying attention. We keep watch so we don't get lost with random thoughts. Quiet gives way to calm. In the calm, we train our minds and bodies to become familiar with the experience. When calm in mind and body, we notice a connection to an understanding and creative energy that we don't achieve during chatter and drama of an unskillful mind.

Over the next week, add three minutes to the seven of last week, increasing your sitting time to ten minutes. Continue counting the breath cycles and notice the development of quiet. Observe the thoughts and bring your focus back to the breath. Notice inner reactions to thoughts. Observe them with curiosity. If they upset you, feel it and bring attention to your breath. Notice the emotions and sensations of your body. If thoughts make you happy, notice it. How does it feel? What is happening in your body and your mind?

Remember, these are only feelings usually induced by chemicals released from the body such as endorphins or cortisol. And, of course, random thoughts mixed with more thoughts that continue to arise. Don't react one way or the other, positively or negatively. Just notice them and return your attention to the breath. When in doubt, always focus on the breath.

To this point, you have been counting the breath cycles like this:

As you breathe in, count "one," breathe out, count "one;" breathe in, count "two," breathe out, count "two;" breathe in, count "three," breathe out, count "three." Continue until the tenth count and repeat.

Your mind should be quieter now compared to a couple of weeks ago when you first started. Going forward from here, we count only on the out-breath, like this:

Breathe in, as you breathe out, count "one;" breathe in, as you breathe out, count "two;" breathe in, as you breathe out, count "three." Continue until the tenth count and repeat.

If you find it difficult counting only on the out-breath, continue counting as you were until you become more accustomed to removing the count on the in-breath. The entire process that we establish in this book is to slowly and methodically give the mind less area in which to play. The more we draw in the reins of the mind, the greater it will become a powerful tool for our success and betterment.

As an alternative to counting breath cycles from one to ten, some find using the following four words over two breath cycles to be more powerful for their meditation practice.

Begin on the first cycle by thinking "appear" as you inhale, and "disappear" as you exhale. During the second cycle, think "change" as you inhale, and "new" as you exhale. With this method, you are thinking each word to yourself midpoint into the breath. Depending on your preference, you can try both methods and figure out which of the two works best for you. In both scenarios, remember not to engage thoughts and simply release them with the word "thought."

One who does not motivate oneself when it is time to start — even the young and strong — full of ignorance, whose drive and mind are weak, this lazy and idle individual will find it difficult to attain true knowledge.
— Dhammapada 280

Mindfulness And The Body

*"You cannot rise beyond the external as well as internal reality
unless you understand your own perception."* — *Roshan Sharma*

Now you are becoming more aware of your breath. You may notice things you hadn't before about your physical experience. Perhaps you are aware of soreness, discomfort, numbing, or other sensations like itching or a sneeze. This is a good sign. It means you are more attuned to your physical experience.

Many of us avoid or neglect physical sensations rather than observing them. This may be from a busy mind or due to mental conditioning. Some may exaggerate certain physical experiences to the point of obsession and overthinking.

Maybe you slouch when engaged or get caught up in your work. Mindfulness gives you the skill to check and adjust your posture and supports you to ease discomfort. By frequently scanning your body and maintaining awareness of physical sensations, you support your body and mind in healthy activity.

Just as with the mental experience, we want to be aware of the physical experience—the sensations. The sensations referred to here are standard, everyday physical experiences and sensations such as breeze on the skin, feeling full, or discomfort and numbness of the limbs from sitting too long. Although important elements, they should not be the focal point. We should notice them but return awareness to the breath. This, of course, should not be done to cause or exacerbate physical complications that require medical attention. If you have questions concerning this, first, seek professional medical advice.

Sense Receptors

Let's look at each of the sense receptors through which we receive information and experience life. We receive all stimuli from the inner and outer worlds through the sense receptors. We filter experiences through the mind and this is how we experience life. The mind, or brain, is a sense receptor, but we can also think of it as the body's motherboard.

The sense receptors are:

- The eyes (vision, image)

- The ears (hearing, sound)

- The nose (smell, scent)

- The tongue (taste, flavor)

- The body (touch, feeling)

We filter information from the five receptors mentioned above through the mind—the brain. Consider receiving an excess of random information into the different receptors. The outcome is stress when the brain has a sensory overload. Think about a time when you found yourself in a chaotic situation and a loud sound caused you to respond abnormally forcefully. This reaction was likely the tipping point caused by a buildup of stress already present.

An untrained mind lacks awareness and skills to filter and respond to an excess of information and stimuli. When the untrained mind experiences excessive pressure as sensory input, we encounter high levels of stress and anxiety. This is the reason we need to train our minds to pay attention and be aware of sensory perceptions from experiences like emotional reactions, sights, and sounds — the input we receive through the five sense receptors: the eyes, ears, nose, tongue, and body.

Familiarize yourself with the experience of the sense receptors over the next five weeks, allowing a week for each. Pay attention and notice the varied experiences. You may think, "when am I not aware of these?" In fact, most people don't realize how much we don't notice. Most of us spend a lot of our time on auto-pilot, going about our lives, unaware of what is happening in or around us. Much of life passes us by as we focus on the dialogue and stories in our heads.

Editor's Pick

Everything that we experience is experienced from within.

Sense Receptor Familiarization

As you complete the above-mentioned exercise over the next five weeks, let go of thoughts that try to interfere with the practice. Recognizing internal responses and reactions to input is an essential aspect of mindfulness. When interacting with pleasant versus unpleasant experiences, notice the thoughts as they arise. Notice the emotional and physical responses. Realize how these interactions affect you in positive and negative ways.

Start by digging deeper and ponder the reasons behind the reactions. Forge your way through any push-back and what you discover may surprise you, even help you understand some of your quirks. Consider using a diary or notebook to jot down anything that you notice or stands out. Later on, return to your journal and make note of changes you see in your perception.

While observing your experiences, recognize that all the experiences we perceive are from within. Nothing is without. It is impossible to experience anything in the universe outside our awareness or our internal world. Everything that we experience is experienced from within.

To support sharp awareness, I coordinated each sense receptor to a specific color. To prepare for the next five weeks of sense receptor practice, gather five pieces of string that you can wear on your wrist or anything of that color. This reminds you to pay attention to the sense receptor of that color during the week. You may even wear clothing of that color during the week or come up with an alternative for the week's corresponding color to remind you to practice.

The following are the colors in correspondence to its sense receptor:

- yellow - eyes

- green - ears

- white - nose

- red - tongue

- blue – body

Five Weeks to Deeper Awareness

Week One—Mindful Vision (yellow)

During our waking hours, our eyes constantly take in a hefty amount of information. The mind will then filter the visual information based on the level of importance, essentially deciding what to pay attention to and what to ignore. Or, so we think.

Here is where applying mindfulness is important. Many times, when we aren't applying mindfulness, we may not notice something that we should, or we may focus too much on something that we should not. Either way, it depends on our ability to control our line of sight and manage our field of vision.

There are a lot of visual objects and details we don't notice. Many times, when looking at something, we don't really see it. We think we see it but it doesn't register the information of what is there: detail, color, texture, or completeness. This is because we take for granted seeing things from a glance on the surface. Since there is so much to see, we may not really see anything of significance.

When aware of how influential it is to notice what we see, we can interact and respond to it better, rather than react. Let's say, for instance, you see something you like. You will most likely have a positive reaction, a clinging desire to continue looking at it. "I like this, I want more." However, when we see something we don't like, we may react by trying to push it away or change it. "I don't like this, I want it to go away." Thus, it's important to pay attention to the different reactions we have in situations and notice the underlying reasons as to why.

For the next week, practice *mindful vision*. Begin by finding something you are familiar with like something you have looked at frequently before. Maybe a wall, a street, or anything familiar.

After you complete at least five minutes of quiet meditation, spend a couple of minutes observing the object while continuing to focus awareness on the breath.

What do you notice that you had not noticed before? Any details or variations? Although you are familiar with the object, you may not have noticed certain details or characteristics about it had you not been applying mindfulness. Note what you saw and jot it down in your journal.

Over the next week, remember to wear yellow or find an alternative to keep the color yellow within view as a reminder for you to practice *mindful vision*.

Week Two—Mindful Hearing (green)

Our ears are constantly busy picking up sounds from every direction. We hear without thinking. Our hearing is on autopilot more often than not. Just as with the eyes, the brain filters sounds within the hearing range. So many sounds go unnoticed but when we are aware of sounds that we had not noticed or paid much attention to before, we may discover new fascinations in the world.

Most of us notice sounds that are closer in range or ones we are more sensitive to, such as a mother hearing a crying child. How do we react to the honk of a car horn, an emergency vehicle, the ringtone of our cellphone, or a doorbell? These sounds are the kinds of notifications that we condition ourselves to notice. On the contrary, what about ambient sounds, sounds of nature, things going on around us like sounds in the environment?

We may also listen to sounds in our bodies such as sounds of digestion, air as it escapes from the stomach, a cough, or a sneeze. Perhaps the cracking sound of a joint, rubbing an ear, or the sound of teeth chattering.

Many times, when we are in a zone of high engagement with something, we may not notice sounds around us. The mind blocks out these ambient sounds. However, we can notice these sounds without letting them distract us with the knowledge of knowing which sounds to respond to, including when or how.

Practicing *mindful hearing* is a positive thing to do during conversations and meetings. Focus on what the speaker is saying. Listen mindfully. Notice the thoughts that arise during their discourse and ground in the breath while listening. When we focus on the person speaking and not our thoughts or response, we will hear more. This enables us to respond in a way that is most beneficial for the conversation.

During week two, as you meditate daily, apply *mindful hearing* by focusing on your breath and listening for the sounds that are far away. Depending on where you are meditating, the sounds you hear will vary. It could be the sound of a ventilation system, but other times it could be the sounds of birds or the wind rustling through the trees.

We rarely think about the diversity of nature. For instance, when we hear the chirping of birds, we may not consider that this is not the same bird that was chirping yesterday. Most likely, each bird or animal we hear outside is not the same that we had heard previously. Nature has so many sounds that we take for granted, like the sound of the wind or the rain. Notice details and characteristics of each experience as if it's the first time you experienced it.

Listen for the sounds that are far away. Train your mind to hear sounds furthest from you, giving less attention to ones that are near. This will help you become more aware of your surroundings. As you sit at your desk or work on a project, you will notice the sounds and expand your awareness organically as you maintain focus on the breath.

During the week of this practice, be sure to wear green or design some way to keep the color green within easy view as a reminder for you to practice *mindful hearing*.

Week Three—Mindful Smell (white)

We have engaged the nose since the beginning of our meditation practice. The nose is the focal point for meditation. It is the point where we focus on the breath cycle — in-breath and out-breath. We sense the cool air as we breathe in and warm air as we breathe out. We may notice the sensation of the breath on the tip of the nose and the upper lip. This is a central tenet to meditation practice and is also applied to a mindfulness practice. When working hard at our desks, possibly experiencing anxiety from a deadline, we want to focus our attention on the tip of the nose, nostrils, or belly. This is done to connect with the breath and be more focused on the task.

We experience a world of smells, odors, and aromas through the nose. When we smell something, it sends a message to our brains. We may all react differently to different scents. Right now, think of a smell you like. If it's food, do you salivate when you think about it? Do you notice a desire? What if the smell is unpleasant? Do you wave your hand in front of your nose? Do you avoid the odor? We all react to things from conditioning caused by previous experiences or situations. Maybe the smell is new to you but you still have information to refer to in your mind that will categorize the smell into a group that gets different reactions. These categories are most likely some variance of "like" or "dislike."

Over the third week, practice *mindful smelling*. Throughout that week, take time to smell many different things, some familiar and some not. Notice what you smell and experience it for its innate qualities, avoiding judgment as pleasant or unpleasant. Mix it up. Smell things that you are familiar with, things that aren't, things that would spark desire, or even ones you would avoid. Do it mindfully. While smelling odors throughout the week, connect with your breath and notice your inner dialogue and emotional reactions. Smelling certain scents also causes the release of endorphins into our system, a natural hormone found in the brain that makes us feel happy when released. A popular endorphin-releasing scent you might want to experiment with is vanilla, but experiment with a range of smells and notice the reactions in your body and mind.

Learning to become aware of inner reactions to smells helps us become aware of physical and mental reactions in other situations. If the smell is pleasant, try smelling it only as the smell and avoid attaching pleasant thoughts to it. Keep it basic. Just let it be "a smell" with no other labels. The same goes for a smell that you find unpleasant. Allow yourself to smell it without judgment, remove labels, and simply notice the qualities of the smell. What are some qualities that you notice? Use descriptive words that don't carry judgment, such as sweet, sour, musky, or pungent. While doing this, notice personal insights and jot them down in your notebook.

Over the week of this practice, be sure to wear white or design some way to keep the color white within easy view as a reminder for you to practice *mindful smell*.

Week Four – Mindful Tasting (red)

Taste is a powerful sense. It supports our need to eat. If we can't taste, we will not enjoy eating. The nose also supports the taste experience. Most of us know, when our nose is stuffy, food is not as flavorful. When we taste or smell something we enjoy, it sends signals to our brains that cause a release of endorphins into our system. Certain foods are more apt to cause a release of endorphins than others. Most flavors can be categorized into the basic four: sweet, sour, bitter, and salty.

Similar to the *mindful smell*, practice sensitivity to a variety of tastes and flavors. Focus on your breath while you eat and slow down the eating process. Most of us don't chew enough times to really taste the food. Try slowing down and chewing more than you are used to.

You may notice that despite the fact you want to chew more, your body is accustomed to only chewing so many or few times before the tongue and throat begin anticipating to move the food toward the stomach. Noticing these types of underlying thoughts and reactions requires a focused and sharp mind. If you haven't reached that sensitivity yet, you will still observe other reactions and thoughts that are more noticeable as your sensitivities increase.

Notice the flavors. Do they change when you chew more than less? Chewing more is good for our digestive systems and better nutrient absorption. So, it is a good habit to adopt.

During the week of this practice, be sure to wear red or design some way to keep the color red within easy view as a reminder for you to practice *mindful tasting*.

Simple Mindful Eating Practice

Mindful eating is a good way to notice the reactions of the body and mind brought on by tastes. Plan to do this as a sitting meditation practice. I suggest you prepare a few chocolate chips or raisins to use during the practice.

1. Sit as you would for regular meditation and take a few minutes to ground yourself in the breath.

2. Pick up a chocolate chip or raisin and smell it for 15 – 30 seconds. What physical or mental reactions do you notice?

3. Now, place it on your tongue. Don't chew, just set it on your tongue for 30 seconds to a minute. Notice any physical or mental reactions or changes. What is happening?

4. Take one bite. Don't chew. Hold that for 30 seconds. What are you experiencing?

5. Now, chew slowly. Focus on the breath and notice the experience.

6. When ready, you can swallow. Now, sit quietly and contemplate the experience. Jot it down in your notebook.

Week Five – Mindful Body (blue)

When we talk about *mindful body*, it entails a lot of real estate. It incorporates the largest bodily organ — the skin. The body gives us a lot of areas to focus on and will take time to become accustomed to paying attention to the many aspects of the body. Take your time. The body can experience many sensations such as an itch, pinch, pain, tickle, warmth, cold, flush, and much more. When considering the internal body, there is also a large quantity of sensations that we can experience such as twitches, joint pain, a scratchy throat, muscle stiffness and soreness, or even sensations from liquids and food that we swallow.

Awareness of sensation is a large part of the bodily experience. As always, maintain awareness of the breath cycles—breathing in and out. In one full breath cycle, notice the cool air of the in-breath contrasted with the warmer out-breath. Notice your belly expanding and contracting. Maybe you notice less tensing of the diaphragm muscles as belly breathing has become more natural.

Slowly, practice expanding awareness to your whole body. Sit quietly. Sense as many body parts as possible. Attempt to encompass your whole body and practice experiencing it as one unit in your mind. This may take some time, but it is a valuable practice in mind-training.

At first, like a body scan, start from a preferred area of your body and slowly expand your awareness to encompass its entirety. Take in as much as you can at first and continue the practice as you expand awareness. By doing so, your body scans will also become quicker and more effective.

Eventually, you will be able to accomplish a body scan instantaneously by bringing your whole body into your scope of awareness and noticing areas that need relaxation on the out-breath including tension that needs to be released or posture needing adjustment.

Practice increasing sensitivity to a variety of sensations. Notice sensations and feelings you experience outside your cognitive awareness. This could be anything from a slight breeze or draft that brushes against your skin or an internal bodily process. Notice the sensation of water on your skin and how your mind reacts to different temperatures. This is something that can be easily performed while showering or washing your hands.

Some sensations you notice may be a form of soreness, pain, or muscle tension. Focusing on and breathing into these areas may help relieve the uncomfortable sensations. Release the discomfort with the out-breath. Notice and return focus to the breath. Avoid judging and simply notice them as a sensation. Notice the mental reactions and any labeling processes as you practice.

Always practice in a way that is in line with the advice of medical professionals. Never disregard situations where medical treatment should be sought out.

Over the week of this practice, wear the color blue or design some way to keep the color blue within easy view as a reminder for you to practice *mindful body*.

The Mind (purple)

The sixth *Sense Receptor* is the mind. The mind is the most difficult and most powerful of them all. It is the force behind our thoughts and how we perceive reality.

The Dhammapada explains aspects of the mind well.

All that we are is the result of what we have thought: all is founded on our thoughts, and made up of our thoughts. If one speaks or acts with an evil thought, pain follows, as the wheel follows the foot of the ox pulling a cart.

All that we are is the result of what we have thought: all founded on our thoughts, and made up of our thoughts. If one speaks or acts with pure thought, happiness follows, like a shadow that never departs. Dhammapada 1-2

The mind is constantly at the core of the six receptors as it plays a major role in the controlling and conducting of all six. It is important, however, that we are the ones in control of the mind.

During week six, practice combining all six of the sense receptors and pay close attention to the thoughts and emotions that emanate from within the mind.

Bringing the Colors Together

While working through each of the five weeks to deeper awareness, your mind will naturally notice things from previous weeks of practice. For example, in the first week, you worked on eyes (yellow) and in the following, you are working on ears (green). As you practice *mindful hearing* throughout the following week, you may find that you also notice things that are related to *mindful vision* from the previous week. This is wonderful. It shows you are on the path to incorporating the practices into your awareness and allowing them to occur organically.

As you continue to practice, they will become second nature. You will notice things and maintain expanded awareness in a quiet and mindful internal space, all the while engaged in the moment.

You have begun establishing an underlying flow of awareness that creates a foundation for focus and grounding. This leads to enhanced mood, productivity, and relationships.

All in all, this is the new normal — awareness of the six sense receptors, their interactions, and influences on your every moment.

He who formerly was reckless and afterwards
became sober, brightens up this world, like the
bright moon freed from the cover of clouds.
— Dhammapada 172

The Wisdom Of Change

"The world as we have created it is a process of our thinking. It cannot be changed without changing our thinking."
— *Albert Einstein*

Nothing can exist without change. Nothing can survive without change. When we watch the cycles of nature, we see the most blatant expression of change in the seasons.

Fall is the season where we observe the seasonal dying of plant and insect life. It is the period when animals prepare for hibernation in expectation of the forthcoming coldest days of the year. Spring, on the other hand, is the most celebrated season in human traditions. Celebrations around the spring season are found worldwide. Most of these celebrations are based on old and long-standing traditions. Although many have lost their truest essence, they are still celebrated, some within smaller communities.

The main reason for these celebrations is to rejoice at the return of warmer days, fresh green grass, and beautiful flowering plants, all of which are an ageless sign to humanity that sustenance will once again become plentiful.

In today's world, many seem less aware of the profound meaning of seasonal changes. Modern humanity is only slightly affected by these transitions as we have lost much of our innate connection with nature.

Of course, many times, we see these seasonal changes from the comfort of our homes. We judge them from a perspective of their direct influence, be it ease or difficulty, on our daily lives. We fail to notice these transitions from a mindful place of acceptance and space of non-judgment, simply acknowledging its importance.

Observe the Change

Change is a huge component of our existence. From our first breath to the last, change is the one constant in our lives. It's also one thing that many become conditioned to dislike and is not easily accepted by all. However, it is something we should all embrace at the core.

Recognizing that change is constant and not static is the first step to finding peace of mind and happiness in life. Take, for instance, losing a dear friend. You have an empty place in your heart that no one else can fill. The ripple effect is easy to imagine considering the influence the emotional pain has on our life responses.

In today's material-driven world, money is also a big factor. With media outlets touting "perfection" and success achieved in ways that don't blend with reality or the constant push for more, it becomes a steeper uphill battle. Without the tools to travel the arduous journey, many fail.

The Chinese expression, "静观其变 In silence, observe the change," we are advised to be calm and observe the happenings in our lives and the change that follows.

Balancing change requires grounding, insight, and sensitivity. Sometimes, we find ways to work with change. Other times, we may need to practice accepting change. The worst response, on the other hand, is to fight it. When we do this, we exhaust ourselves and exert counterproductive energy back into the universe. This can have a negative effect on our lives and situations, magnifying the ripple effect.

When we consider the expression, "In silence, observe the change," silence is the proper state for learning, observance is the key to understanding, and a sense of contentment is the fruit of acceptance. When the outcome is not as we hoped, we realize the wisdom of change. Through acceptance, we find contentment beyond understanding.

When applying mindfulness to challenging situations or changes, we become more aware of the acute nuances of change. We then learn the power of acceptance. In other words, don't get caught up in the thought process that leads us down a rabbit hole, culminating in emotional and physical anguish. By applying mindfulness and grounding ourselves in the breath, we are more aware and accepting of the ebb and flow of change with the realization that nothing is static. Things change. One friend is gone, another will arrive.

Many times, what happens is, we get caught up in the emotions of a situation. Anger, frustration, fear, anxiety — a variety of reactions to situations we approach with a negative attitude such as, "this is not what I want," or, "this is not good." When we label situations with such words, they create emotional deep reactions. If we aren't mindful, we will end up in a position less conducive to achieving the outcomes we hope for. Much like operating systems running our computers, the subconscious mind can have a stronghold on our lives creating turmoil and challenges at every turn. The inner reactions to words and the emotions that bubble up from deep inside our minds are some of the more challenging experiences we deal with. They are the things we need to attend to most if we want to advance toward our potential.

I used to have anger issues. It was like a fire inside my stomach that would explode uncontrollably when triggered. Insecurities were constantly whispering destructive words from the edges of my mind. Fears and conditioning would raise their heads at any given moment to push me back into the muck of my own making.

For many of us, the words and phrases that reside in our minds shape who we are. The unskillful ones constantly showing their faces keep us locked in a place of submission to words, phrases, and ideas that support a destructive inner story. Without changing the inner story, we cannot achieve constructive change in our lives to give us a chance at becoming the best version of ourselves we are meant to be.

If you want to change your body, it takes consistent and persistent work. We all know that real change requires real effort. The same is true for the mind. When we want to improve our lives, we must be able to pay attention so we can see what is going on in our heads and begin the process of change.

Change is the key to success and acceptance is
the key to successful change.

Please read that a few times before continuing.

If you feel stressed, just feel it. Don't react to it! Don't make stress, frustration, or anything destructive, for that matter, a topic of your conversations or inner dialogues. This is where mindfulness comes in. Notice the self-undermining dialogues in your head, raise red flags over them, then, return focus to your breath.

Notice the length and characteristics of each breath. This may sound strange, but as you become more acquainted with your breath by paying more attention to it, you will notice slight variations and aspects of the breath that you had not before. In fact, the practice of focusing and grounding yourself in the breath leads to realizations that you never noticed before. This could be considered a form of enlightenment, something most people misunderstand. Something akin to a sudden wave of otherworldly realization, however, this is not necessarily true. Enlightenment is an incremental process directly connected to the subtle awareness of mindfulness based on a calm and quiet heart-mind.

To Think or Not to Think

Thinking is not an option any more than breathing or a beating heart. The brain thinks. That's what it does. It won't stop until it ceases getting oxygen.

Now, this isn't to say cognition, or thinking, can't be slowed down or quieted. There is no way to completely shut it off. Not to mention, this probably wouldn't be a good idea. However, when we are able to quiet brain activity, we can connect better with our true self and our thought processes.

The brain is like a recorder that documents and remembers information. Similar to those aggravating pop-up ads on the web, the subconscious mind may randomly toss thoughts into the conscious mind at any time. These thoughts can sometimes be frustrating or they may catch our attention and carry us off into a branching of thoughts with no rhyme or reason. They seemingly come from left field, triggered by a word, image, or sound. Anything can trigger a memory, even a visceral experience expressed through a thought.

I love the phrase, "I am not my thoughts and my thoughts are not me." It's quite liberating to consider this novel idea. How many of us have felt badly over something that crossed our minds? I remember wondering if something was wrong with me, even questioning if I was a bad person, simply from the thoughts that coursed through my head. Now, however, I realize that this is not the case and that the brain is a random thought-tossing machine.

Since those times of second-guessing my own character, I have taken control. I do the thinking that I used to leave to the brain. Although, at times, it's still conniving and inserts wanton thoughts vying for my attention to pull me off track when I'm not vigilant. Thus, it's imperative to manage our thoughts and not let them derail us. This is done by maintaining awareness by paying attention. Only then am I able to keep my thoughts on the right track.

Again, thinking is not an option. However, managing the thoughts I engage in and the ones I let go of is my choice.

The Progression of Thoughts

Thoughts will come, but at times, they appear like a storm. One thought can trigger an avalanche in the mind. If these thoughts are destructive, angry, fearful, or form low vibrational emotions, they most likely do not lead to positive and uplifting results. These are the thoughts that we want to be aware of. These are the thoughts that cause us to do, feel, think, or say things that we may regret.

Of course, not all happy thoughts are good either. Consider the arrogant person who only talks about themselves and how great they are. This is the result of a self-consumed mind. These are also destructive thoughts tempting us to become enamored with ourselves with seeds of selfishness, greed, and a sense of entitlement.

We strive to keep these thoughts and emotions at bay and in check. This is done by constant awareness of the thoughts in the mind and by practicing awareness of the emotions they trigger. Once we allow the emotions to kick in, we're fighting an uphill battle.

The sooner we notice these unskillful thoughts and emotions, the sooner we can release them with the out-breath and let them move on. These emotional thought expressions pull us down and emit negative harmful energy into our relations and daily lives. If you notice a destructive thought similar to, "I hate that person," or, "I'm better at this than they are," replace it with, "I love that person," or, "We are both good at this, we just have a different approach."

As for the word "hate," I always avoid dropping the "H" bomb. Even using the word to express a casual attitude toward a place or thing still embodies powerful negative energy.

Seductive and enticing thoughts can be an even bigger challenge. These thoughts draw us in and captivate us because we enjoy them. They make us feel good as we get drawn into their mesmerizing allure. These kinds of thoughts take advantage of our ruminating weaknesses of cravings and other desires.

When seductive thoughts pop into our awareness, we should treat them the same as destructive thoughts. The untrained mind draws in and pushes away. It draws in the enticing and seductive thoughts and pushes away things that it doesn't find desirable. This is why we have knee-jerk reactions to things we don't like almost as if we didn't even think about it. One thing is for sure, we weren't aware of it until the damage was done. Craving and desire are the same. We get caught up in the process of the thoughts and take the bait.

Paying attention and being aware is imperative when it comes to managing thoughts. When we notice emotional thoughts, positive or negative, they can become a trap for the untrained mind.

Now, what if we fall for the bait? Well, that is bound to happen and the first thing to do is, much like losing track of your count when completing the breath cycle exercise, simply, start over. Forget the mistake and move on. Of course, just like the counting mishap, we want to examine the reason why it happened so we can step up our game with the mind and better understand its tricks and habits.

Self-compassion is vitally important to successful mindfulness practice. When we are easier on ourselves, we are able to recognize our imperfections without causing self-torture after each mistake. Sequentially, we learn to offer that same self-compassion to our interactions with others through understanding.

Over time, this simple practice increases the quality of relationships and interactions. It will also improve our interpersonal skills. As you perfect and embrace this practice, you will be astounded as it permeates and engages the many aspects of your life.

The Gap Between the Thoughts

I like the phrase, "Focus on the gap between the thoughts." It holds a lot of perspectives that allow us to consider the gaps included in thoughts. These gaps are what we consider the quiet space, which is what we want to focus on.

When we focus on the quiet space between thoughts, we are more apt to make that our focus rather than the thoughts themselves. Therefore, we tend to give thoughts less attention than the gaps between them. When we achieve this, we are able to engage the thoughts we choose and we are more in touch with our core self. This is the space from which improved creative skills and new ideas spawn. Creativity arises from the silence of the mind, not the chatter.

During a barrage of thoughts, the gap is more difficult to find. If that is the case, bring the focus back to the breath and change the focus of the mind's eye. Nudge it back to the breath. When you are struggling with thoughts and the mind, begin counting breath cycles.

Thoughts can be difficult to control and they can also be sneaky, almost evasive. I've experienced meditations where it felt like a battle was taking place in my head. The mind was pushing thoughts on me that I didn't want to pay attention to. It felt like I had to rip attention away from the things the mind thrust at me. I grounded myself by counting the breath cycles. It will continue to happen but eventually, the mind weakens.

Once we have begun experiencing the newfound quiet, we continue pushing forward. Eventually, focusing on the good becomes second nature, and the mind quiets.

Quieting the Mind

Quieting the mind is a process that takes time. There is no specific amount of time because each person is different and will apply different amounts of energy to their practice. If your meditation is comfortable and enjoyable, it is very unlikely you will experience many transformations. If you, on the other hand, are willing to push yourself by increasing how often you sit to meditate, along with mindful thought practices throughout your day, you will experience a greater amount of transformation. The important thing is to continue pushing yourself if you want to experience amazing change in your life.

Establishing a daily meditation ritual and sticking with it is the first and most important thing to do to quiet your mind. A quiet mind is the foundation for many facets including better focus and improved productivity. When we work with a quiet mind, we don't have all the distractions of a chatty one. We are able to sit, focus on the task at hand, and get it done with time to spare. Applying a quiet mind through mindfulness practice is a great way to manage time.

Set a daily routine and be sure to stick with it. You will realize how the mind continually brings up things to do or questions about what you are doing. This is the time to keep your focus solely on the breath. Follow the breathing and count the breath cycles.

If you stop your meditation routine or falter for some time, certainly, it will be a challenge to achieve the meditation you had been performing when you return. In this case, we essentially have to rebuild the practice. The process is not enjoyable but it has to be done.

Meditating daily is the most important aspect of establishing an effective practice, even at your leisure at any given place. Waiting for a connecting flight as I traveled across the Pacific, I frequently sought out an obscure area in the airport, sat on my coat or shoes, and meditated. I was aware of people walking around me, the announcements over the PA system, along with the variation of sounds and sensations surrounding me. Nonetheless, I was still able to complete my meditation. Always taking time to meditate and focus on the breath is important.

Find the Space Between the Fish

Imagine standing in a pool of water up to your neck. You stand still. There are fish swimming around you. Now, imagine that the pool is your mind in the present moment and the fish represent your thoughts. Eventually, some of the fish will brush up against you and you will become aware of the fish. "Oh, a fish just brushed up against me."

You could become engaged with the fish and wonder where it went, if it will brush up against you again, or even question if it bites. Alternatively, you can simply continue standing in the water quiet in the present moment.

In the same way, a thought comes into your mind, you notice it, now, let it move on. Don't engage in it. Of course, in the case of the fish, you may anticipate a fish close by and wonder if one will brush against you again or how many are in the pond.

This is much how thoughts are. They are there, swimming around, and they never stop swimming because the brain is the home to thoughts. The difference is not how many there are or if they are there or not. The difference is in how we anticipate, interact with, and engage the thoughts.

Be still. The thoughts are always there, bumping against the walls of our mind, leaving us with a choice. The choice to engage or disengage.

When standing in the pond, we want to focus on the space between the fish. When we focus on the space between the fish, we are focusing on the present moment—the quiet, calm space.

The same can be done with thoughts. Find the space between the thoughts and focus on that space. Keep your attention and awareness on the space between the thoughts. When another thought appears, nip it in the bud before it has the chance to complete itself. Stay in the space between the thoughts. This will increase focus and the ability to complete tasks and get things done. Not to mention, it will give you that extra buffer of time to respond better in stressful situations. Focusing on the space between the thoughts will keep your attention on the things that need to be attended to in the moment.

Like-Minded Friends and Family

Surround yourself with people who push you to become a better expression of self. Those who are the image of who you want to become.

Finding individuals who resonate with our personal concept of "a better me," are the types of people we want to surround ourselves with. Humans are community-oriented. We want to be accepted and be a member of a community. The community that we spend our time with is the one that we will learn and grow from.

Similar to our thoughts creating our reality, the people we spend our time with also have a strong influence on who we are.

If we hang out with people who challenge us to be a better person, we have a support system in them to fall back on. If we surround ourselves with people who pull us down and make us weak, we will have a difficult time finding the energy to overcome.

Choose wisely the people you associate with and learn from as it could be a matter of success or failure. Learn compassion and acceptance, and distance yourself from anger and hatred. Look for and see similarities, not differences. See the good in all.

By doing so, you achieve the fine line of balance in your awareness. You will experience improved relationships, increased effectiveness, and a deeper sense of purpose.

You will also experience profound wisdom and increased productivity, the road to inner peace, and the thread of universal connection that touches your life.

Like a beautiful and fragrant flower that grows near trash discarded on the highway, the practitioner of the enlightened stands out among those who are weak in mind, the people that walk in darkness.

— Dhammapada 58-59

The Yin-Yang Of Acceptance

"When [the] waxing and waning of yin-yang can be kept within a certain range, degree, and period, ... things will be in a relatively stable state."
–DongPei Hu, Traditional Chinese Medicine:
Theory and Principles

Like the weather, life is always changing. Nothing is static. We wake up in the morning, welcoming the daylight. Experiencing the progression of the day, we rarely consider the incremental transition from dawn to daylight, and dusk to night. And we are no more attuned to the waxing and waning moon that lights the night sky.

In life, change is inevitable. Yet, in some ways, our culture leads us to believe that things don't change, or that change is bad, suggesting it would be better to keep things static. Various worship beliefs offer the promise of security that, after death, we may arrive in a static world where we will no longer be concerned or fearful of change. This mindset instills in some the desire for a static, unchanging existence, which, when looking around, goes against everything we observe in nature and reality. Unfortunately, this desire pushes one deeper into the illusive mind, seeking to create an illusory existence of "perfection." It nudges one into illusions of faultlessness.

When you look at your surroundings, what do you see that does not experience change through aging, oxidation, rusting, depreciation, or wilting? Nothing. The universe, and everything in it, is in constant flux. Things constantly chip away, break down, and renew, all throughout the process of death. The earth experiences renewal from the dying and decomposing of living organisms and the human body experiences renewal through cells dying and regenerating.

As the outside world changes, so does our inner world. Reflect on the moods one experiences in a day as thoughts wax and wane, creating changes in our minds. We change opinions, preferences, and distastes, all without batting an eye. Some of these changes are by choice caused by the lack of acceptance for natural change, or simply, a need for self-expression.

On the contrary, what about the changes we don't choose? Instances such as losing a pet, loss of a job opportunity, or the death of a loved one. How do we adjust to this change? How do we respond and foster contentment? How do we maintain balance when change is just around the corner? The concept of yin-yang offers us insights to manage and balance experiences through understanding the makeup of life and its phenomena.

Yin-Yang Oneness

Let's recap and go more in depth into yin-yang. As mentioned in previous chapters, yin-yang is the traditional Chinese perception of all that we see and experience. It is a universal code to understanding existence as we know it.

Most of us have heard of yin-yang at some point. Some may think of it as female and male, dark and light, or black and white, however, it's not that simple. They are correct, but only to a superficial extent. As you have come to understand, the Yi Jing, better known in the West as the Book of Changes, extends the concept of yin-yang far beyond a simple black and white.

The earliest description of yin-yang is expressed as "yin," the shady side of a mountain, and "yang," the sunny side. Together, these two elements are the basis of a complete worldview that we can apply to all experiences.

In the West, we built much of our cultural awareness around the idea of "avoidance to change," a concept that everything is best kept static. Consequently, one may dispute the theory that black has components of white, female has components of male, and bad has components of good. When we slow down and observe, we also realize nothing exists of its own accord, an idea referred to as "dependent origination."

Dependent origination is a concept based on the idea of the impossibility for anything to exist without dependency on other forces or phenomena. This is also the most basic meaning of emptiness from a Buddhist perspective. Simply put, life cannot exist without sunlight, water, or oxygen. This can even be narrowed down to our individual dependency on social networks, farmers, friends, and family.

From the perspective of yin-yang, everything that exists has a contrary expression. Life cannot exist without death and happiness cannot exist without sadness. If we don't have black, we cannot have white, and bad does not exist without good. They are each, in fact, opposite expressions of a dualistic whole. We can easily grasp this concept by using the duration of a day as an example. (See figure 9.1)

Most of us do not put much thought into the progression that happens from daytime to night. Although we have the vocabulary in our language to express various incremental changes, such as "dusk" and "dawn," words fail to express the progression. It is easier to see the changes as they take place or in a time-lapse video showing the progression digitally sped up. It offers us a view of the complete cycle of yin (night) transitioning to yang (day).

In nature, there is no definitive division between the progression from night to day, yet we apply words that describe them as two distinct periods. In reality, they are one unit composed of two opposites, which we know to be a whole day, each containing components of the other. Within the whole exists thousands upon thousands of minute changes taking place.

In the above image of the Taiji, more commonly known to be the symbol for yin-yang, it depicts the duration of a whole day. The dots within the two symbolize that each one is present in the opposite. The narrowest points in each half of the symbol represent the gradual transition, or flip, to the other, maintaining the two as one whole.

It is important to understand this cycle in order to apply the concepts to our own lives and experiences. Once we understand the cyclic flow of yin-yang and observe the change, we see the transition in the progression. Sometimes, the clarity is more evident, but the seed of change is present at all times.

Consider the seasons. Most cultures accept that there are four seasons. The four are composed of different combinations of "one yin and one yang." Within each season, there is a seed of change.

There is also a oneness in the whole of the four, a oneness that binds them as a unit made up of yin-yang. Thus, we can easily see yin-yang switching in the four seasonal transitions of spring to summer, summer to fall, fall to winter, and winter to spring.

Editor's Pick

Thus, trust the wisdom of nature. Trust the wisdom of life. Accept the things that come through the natural cycle, both the good and the bad. Understand that it is part of a bigger and more powerful journey than we could ever design for ourselves.

The Chinese Oracle of Wisdom – The Yi Jing

Let's take a deeper look into the idea of yin-yang within the Yi Jing.

In the Yi Jing, Confucius writes, "一阴一阳之谓道," which transliterates the interaction of one yin and one yang as "Dao." The two, one yin and one yang, are not separate or divided, therefore, should be viewed as a single unit.

When we understand how change takes place within yin-yang, we can recognize its influence on life, even if it's not physically visible. Since the Western mindset categorizes, separates, and divides, it may not be as easy to understand the concept of yin-yang as one whole consisting of two expressions. However, by observing and contemplating changes occurring around you, you will become aware of yin-yang transitions at play.

The Beginning of the Yi Jing

The concept of the Yi Jing was initially created over five thousand years ago before China boasted a system of writing. The novel concept started with a single-line symbolism representing "道 Dao," the universe outside of which nothing exists.

The Chinese expression, "一画开天 The single line begets the universe," refers to a single line representing Taiji (太极) or Dao (see figure 9.2). This concept suggests that the Taiji gives way to "the two" — one yin and one yang. Thus, the single line contains all things in the universe — the interaction of yin-yang.

———

Fig. 9.2 The Taiji

Within the idea of "the whole," Taiji relates to anything. This could be a day, a life, a relationship, a career, even an experience.

In figure 9.3 below, we see the "one yin and one yang" makeup of the Taiji where yin is expressed through the divided line and yang through the solid.

— —   ———

Fig. 9.3 One yin and one yang

In the world of Yi Jing, just as plants, animals, and humans grow upward, change ascends. Everything evolves upwards. This relationship between the Taiji and yin-yang can be seen in figure 9.4 where Taiji, the "one," is the beginning, and one yin and one yang as the two opposing non-aggressive expressions that are the makeup of "one" evolve upward.

Fig. 9.4 Taiji is yin-yang

The interactions of yin-yang range far and wide consisting of constant change, movement, and evolution. Yin is described as feminine but is not to be confused as female. It is cool, dark, contracting, concealed, and represents a scoundrel character. Yang, on the other hand, is masculine. It is warm, bright, expanding, exposed, and represents a respectable person. Similar to yin, yang should not be confused as male despite masculinity.

Can one say "dislike" is present in "like?" Of course!

It's important to remember that there is no pure expression. One expression is always influenced by the opposite. Thus, the black and white dots within the yin-yang image remind us that aspects of the opposite are always present to some degree. Thus, there is always some form of "like" within an expression of "dislike."

Understanding the Idea of "the Whole"

Again, it's important to note that there is no separation of yin-yang. Rather, it is a transition where the two harmonize and remain as one. We should refer to the one as "yin-yang," rather than "yin and yang," because the latter creates a sense of division between the two.

As mentioned, the Western mindset has a tendency to divide and separate. This potentially leads us to an incomplete view of the world around us with divisions and separations rather than relations and connections. The Chinese mindset is one of yin-yang connections — cycling relations established on the balance of contrary expressions as described in the Yi Jing. This concept is also prevalent in the Chinese language and permeates the traditional Chinese worldview.

As we gain insight into how yin-yang balances the physical and elemental universe, we see how it influences our lives. From the single line representing the "whole," to the makeup of "the two," it then develops to "the four," which are expressions of natural phenomena we experience daily.

The foundational two-line symbolism of yin-yang, expressed in the familiar black and white fish symbol, then gives way to the following four two-line symbols. These, as with earlier examples, also evolve upwardly.

The first is double-yin which represents the moon or feminine energy, such as deep night and winter. The second is one-yin beneath one-yang representing warm feminine energy in dawn and spring. The third is double-yang which represents the sun or masculine energy, like high noon and summer. Last, the fourth is one-yang beneath one-yin, cool masculine energy into dusk and autumn. (See figure 9.5)

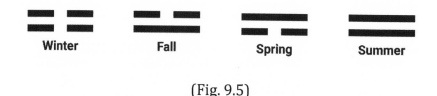

(Fig. 9.5)

Here, we see how these four symbols represent common cyclic universal expressions of four, including seasons and other life and energy cycles. We can also apply this concept to our lives as we observe the passing of days and the ebb and flow of life experiences.

The Yi Jing continues to expand by intermingling one yin and one yang as three-line combinations, developing the eight trigram symbols, each representing aspects of nature – namely heaven, wetlands, fire, lightning, wind, water, mountains, and earth (See figure 9.6). These eight then intermingle again as trigram-pairs to make up the sixty-four hexagrams. With this, everything that comprises the natural world, including life, relationships, and the universal cycles, all find expression in the Yi Jing.

The Yi Jing is a tool for insight. It is an oracle that spawns wisdom and sparks enlightenment beyond the often narrow two-dimensional perspectives social conditioning has cemented us to.

It guides us to observe nature and the cycles of life from both a yin perspective of dark and contracting, and a perspective of yang, one of warmth and expansion. By contemplating the concepts of the Yi Jing, we gain insight into changes, progressions, and potential in our lives, relations, and careers.

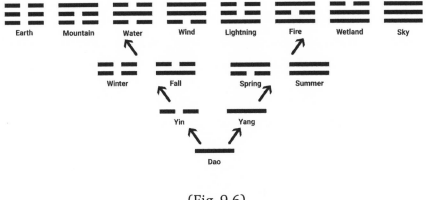

(Fig. 9.6)

The Perfect Balance of Heaven and Earth

The expression, "正乾坤 Perfect Heaven-Earth," refers to the perfect balance between the energies of heaven and earth—yin-yang. When heaven and earth are in balance, we identify its design as an ever-changing, impermanent cycle of forward momentum and development, a response to the energies engaging the moment and circumstances.

Climax Flipping

"物极必反 Climax Flip" – When one energy reaches its pinnacle, it must flip.

If yang energy increases, the progression will develop a stronger yang. We must introduce yin energy to decelerate the increasing yang energy. Not unlike the transition from agitation, a yang energy, to calm, a yin energy. Managing this balance requires sensitivity to the prevalent energy and the wisdom to allow the change to occur. Having reached a climax, a "burn out" will transpire, cycling a climax flip. This may be good or bad, depending on the situation at hand.

Yin-Yang Acceptance

When we consider the different aspects among elements such as day and night, easy and difficult, happy and sad, or hot and cold, we can identify how the interactions between the two illuminate the counterbalance to create their oneness.

Without the harmonizing aspects of the two, the one is not complete and loses equilibrium. They are in constant flow to maintain a balance that is only at an energetic or molecular level, invisible to the naked eye. However, if not well managed, the situation may move into a state of excess, leading to a potentially disruptive climax flip.

During moments when we realize one expression may be overly vigorous, we have the opportunity to balance. For example, when we notice agitated behavior, we will find balance with the counter of passivity. And we notice this shift when we apply the skills of mindfulness.

It is liberating to know that things are in flux. However, if our mindset is one of constant, we may consequently experience mild to severe anxiety, fear, or anger as the flow of change progresses. We should choose from which perspective to view change; from one of static rigidity or flowing transformation. If we don't like change or are afraid of it, then we are living in a place of static rigidity. This is a miserable state to live in. Fearing change would make getting out of bed every day extremely difficult.

When we see change as an opportunity, a space of newness, and a creative force that expands rather than contracts, then our outlook becomes positive, knowing things work for the best. Despite it being for our personal best interest, it will be the best for all, which also comes through the practice of acceptance.

The tougher part may be to maintain a positive outlook and eliminate negative practices, such as labeling things as "bad." It is at this point we remember that bad comprises components of good. By recognizing this, we are better prepared for changes yet to come, seeing them as an expression of either yin or yang, but understanding they also have seeds of the opposite. Realizing this, we see that responding in ways to maintain the flow of "good," without watering the seeds of negativity, may help avoid a potentially undesirable climax flip.

Think about washing a pair of dirty jeans. When you place them in clean water, the water gets dirty. However, we trust the process. We know that when it's finished, the jeans will be clean until they get dirty again. If we stop our thought process and focus only on the dirty water, we may stress that the water is making the jeans more filthy. Understanding how things work and having a good grasp of reality is groundedness. We de-stress when grounded in reality.

But some are afraid of change, which in ways is the social conditioning of our upbringing. It conditioned us to pursue a world where nothing changes and, unrealistically, everything will be perfect — hoping we will get what we want and be with people who will always agree.

Unfortunately, this scenario does not support us to live our current livelihoods. It sprouts a pushback against the reality of our present moment. The reality is that we need to apply proper skills to deal with challenges healthily.

Yet, they have taught us to fight for what we want. In other words, let us not be happy and grateful for what we have in the present. We are told to be the best, but in a group where everyone is told the same, how chaotic will it get? We ought to be the best expression of who *we* are. Each of us possesses unique talents and skills that make us who we are. Focusing on our uniqueness, opposed to individuality, is how we can be the best. To be the best is striving for the best version of ourselves.

The standard pattern established by society is not flexible. It upholds the desire to avoid change and to force-fit within a certain box or prototype. However, neither life nor death can be simplified into a prototype. Nature has its own design and knows better than we. Thus, trust the wisdom of nature. Trust the wisdom of life. Accept the things that come through the natural cycle, both the good and the bad. Understand that it is part of a bigger and more powerful journey than we could ever design for ourselves.

When we accept both the yin and the yang of life's experiences, we lessen undue suffering and discord. It aids in avoiding the struggle of self-induced battles with the flow of life. By observing our lives and the responses we receive from the world around us, we are more capable of learning and harnessing the skills to accept and balance the cycling of yin-yang. By doing so, we experience more peace of mind and exemplify more peace on earth.

As the bee collects nectar without harming the flower, its color or scent, so let us dwell on the earth.

— Dhammapada 49

Tips For Your Mindfulness Practice

The more mindful we are, the more mindful we become. Mindfulness requires consistent application and practice. Thus, it is referred to as "a practice."

Take advantage of all opportunities to practice mindfulness. The more you do, the more habitual it will be. Strive for "mindful without thinking" — a wonderful and powerful idea.

One thing to remember is that all activities and suggestions in this book are rooted in the breath. It is the foundation of a mindful practice. Counting the breath cycles may not always be necessary, but always be aware of the breath as you inhale and exhale.

The following section is a collection of ideas to apply mindfulness in your everyday life.

Mostly, these are methods I have practiced over the years and realize they can be adjusted and applied to different areas. Be creative and open to new ways you can apply mindfulness in your life.

Outdoors

Walking

- Notice your steps. When walking, notice your weight switching from one foot to the other.

- Notice sounds and smells. Be aware of outer physical sensations such as a breeze or the warmth of the sun on your skin.

- Be aware of inner body sensations and your posture.

- Notice your eyes wandering. How does that affect your focus and thinking?

Sitting

- Be aware of your surroundings. Practice mindfulness of vision and hearing. Hear the sounds of nature and notice what sound is farthest from you.

- Notice sensations such as warmth from the sun, a breeze, even insects on your skin.

- Notice life around you, such as animals, insects, plants, and other people. Consider and appreciate their experiences.

In Public

Shopping

- Notice sounds and smells.

- Notice colors and detail.

- Notice your thoughts about the choices and options available to you. How do you respond in your thoughts?

- When standing in line, focus on your breath and notice your posture.

- Notice your eyes wandering. Position them downwards at a 45-degree angle and return focus to your breath. Release any tension or stress with the out-breath.

In the Office

Sitting at Your Desk

- Notice your posture. Be sure you are sitting erect as opposed to slouching.

- Check your breathing. Be sure you are breathing regularly and refrain from holding your breath.

- Be aware of where your feet rest and how they feel. When you move or readjust, apply mindfulness.

- Feel your leg muscles and notice all related sensations.

- Notice your hands. What are they touching? If they are touching your chair, notice the sensation. If they are typing, notice what it feels like. Be aware of any feeling that your hands are experiencing.

- Be aware of the sensation of your buttocks on the chair. If you are standing, notice the balance of your body weight on your feet.

Collaborating or Conversing

- Notice your thoughts. Be aware of thoughts arising. How are they supporting or undermining your endeavors?

- Be aware of reactions. If you are collaborating with others, notice the thought reactions that are arising in your mind. Are they supporting positive conversation?

- Support creativity. Focus your attention on the task and breathe. Relax. The seed of creativity is from a blank slate. Slow the grind of thoughts and ideas. Focus on the space between the thoughts.

- Notice emotions. If you are in a stressful situation, focus your awareness on your feelings. Notice the sensations in your body and the responses in your mind. Don't react. Take one breath and respond.

Meetings or Group Discussions

- Focus on what others are saying. Be aware of your mind planning a response. In this case, bring your attention back to the breath and focus on what is being said. Practice mindful listening.

- When speaking, speak with purpose. Be aware of your thoughts. Are the thoughts and words creating a can of worms?

Focus on the point to be made. There are always opportunities to bring up other points.

The above are only suggestions. Practice and apply them to your needs, surroundings, and lifestyle.

To Cushion or Not to Cushion

Traditionally, meditation is done while sitting on a small rug or cushion. Let's recap and go into more depth of positioning and proper form.

As mentioned in previous chapters, meditation is done in a posture referred to as the "Lotus Position". This is where you sit cross-legged with both feet on the opposite knee. The Half-Lotus is where you sit with only one foot on an opposite knee. Many seem to believe that if you sit in the Lotus Position, you will have a better spiritual experience or that you are a more spiritual practitioner. Nothing could be further from the truth. More than likely, those who express this sentiment base their opinion on a matter of ego.

Meditation is something we can practice anywhere at any time. If we are too concerned about our seated posture, we may not achieve what is most important to meditate. The point of meditation is not to be spiritual, but rather, to be calm and one with the now — the present breath and moment.

There are many benefits of sitting in a traditional posture, however, modifications can be made to allow sitting and meditating in virtually any posture.

The main thing to be aware of is sitting in an erect and respectful manner. Doing so allows us to breathe easily and naturally, which is more important than how we sit. If you can sit in a Full Lotus, that's awesome. If not, try a Half Lotus or the Burmese Posture. Sitting in one of these positions is the best way if you are able.

Sitting Indian Style is not a meditation posture. The reason being is that the knees are not touching the ground. Traditional meditation postures require three points touching the ground, essentially, the buttocks and both knees. This concept can be seen in the Chinese "鼎 Ding," a three-legged vessel for holding liquids.

The importance of maintaining a grounded physical balance is significant and can affect many aspects of a proper meditation practice. The most important of which is in a person's relaxed and meditative state. The body must be anchored and grounded, otherwise, the body may sway or lose balance. When this happens, it could startle the quieted mind.

Therefore, the key to proper posture is to have three points of grounding to support the body in balance.

If you prefer not to sit on a cushion or are physically unable to do so, sitting on a chair is also an option as we mentioned in previous chapters. The best type of chair to use is one that is firm and sturdy, similar to a dining chair. Sofas and overstuffed chairs are not recommended as they are excessively cushioned for meditation.

When you sit on a chair, keep a slight distance from the backrest to avoid leaning your back on it. Place both feet flat on the ground, shoulder-width apart. With your hands relaxed, place it anywhere on your lap that is comfortable and natural. When sitting on a chair, the idea is to achieve the same physical posture with your back as you would sitting on a cushion. The only difference between the two are the positions of your legs. In both scenarios, you want to maintain the same upper-body posture.

Mindfulness on the Go!

Mindfulness on the Go! is a simple daily practice in awareness. Actively practice curiosity using your ears, nose, mouth, eyes, body, and mind/heart. Each day, practice one area. On the seventh day, combine all areas and write down any realizations in your daily journal.

Monday – Ears: Awareness of sounds around you. Which sounds are the farthest from you? Do not label them. Just be aware of the sound. Notice the sounds as if they are inside you.

Tuesday – Nose: Awareness of smells. Don't label them as pleasant or not, be curious about how you interact with them and why. Can you allow the smells to simply be a smell? Also, notice your breathing. Are you breathing into your belly?

Wednesday – Mouth: As you speak, be curious about the words you use and how people respond to them. When eating, take a moment to question whether or not you are actually tasting the food you are eating. In each bite, experience the taste.

Thursday – Eyes: As you look around you, spark curiosity about the things you see. Are they really what they appear to be? When walking, notice aspects of nature around you that you may not have noticed before such as plants, the sky, the position of the sun and the moon. Notice the physical characteristics of people, animals, and objects.

Friday – Body: As you are sitting or walking, notice the pressure and sensations on different areas of your body. While walking, notice the weight on your feet. While sitting, notice the pressure on your buttocks and back. Notice any sensations in your body such as an itch. If you feel such a sensation, experience it for as long as you can.

Saturday – Mind/Heart: As you go about your day, be aware of the thoughts in your mind. If you notice negative talk, change it to positive. Become curious about how things affect you — what people say, how they look at you, how you feel when you are or are not where you want to be. Be curious about where the feeling stems from.

Sunday – This is your opportunity to take all six sense practices you've acquired throughout the week and learn to apply them collectively. Be creative in noticing how they interact and interrelate with one another.

Get curious about internal responses. If you notice anything that you are not comfortable with, just be with it. Don't judge it as right or wrong, good or bad. Simply experience every internal and outer matter with curiosity.

Glossary

A

Action-founded-on-non-action - The idea that non-action is the foundation for action. Only when one embodies non-action are we able to act with balance and control.

Anapanasati - A form of mindful meditation based on awareness of the breath and sensations.

B

Breath (the) - The life-supporting interaction between body, mind, and the inhalation of oxygen-infused air.

Breath cycle - The cyclical concept of in-breath and out-breath, two parts of a whole breath. Breath cycle is based on the concept of Taiji and yin-yang (see, Taiji and yin-yang).

C

Chan 禅 (chán) - A Chinese form of Buddhism based on traditional Buddhist teachings from India. In Japan, it is known as Zen.

D

Dan Tian 丹田 (dān tián) - A location approximately three finger-widths below the navel. In Chinese medicine, it is considered as the location of life energy and warmth within the body.

Dao 道 (dào) - (Tao) A universal concept that grows from the writings of Lao Zi (Laotzu), where Dao is referred to as the force that created the universe, also explained as, "that outside of which nothing exists." The Dao is seen by some to equal the Buddhist concept of Emptiness, and the Judeo-Christian concept of God.

Dao De Jing 道德经 (dào dé jīng) - (Tao Te Ching) The Dao De Jing is the famous writing by the same name. Story has it that Lao Zi left this famous writing with a city gatekeeper as he departed the city for the last time.

Daoism 道教 (dào jiào) - (Taoism) The philosophy built around the writings of Lao Zi that has become a quasi religion.

Dhammapada - (Dharmapada in Sanskrit) The Dhammapada is a collection of sayings by the Buddha Gautama. It is a widely recognized collection of Buddhist thought, similar to the Psalms of the Bible. There are many translations of the Dhammapada.

F

Fu Xi 伏羲 (fú xī) - The mythological first Chinese emperor. Fu Xi is supposed to have lived somewhere around 7000 years ago and is thought to be the creator of foundational Chinese culture, including the Yi Jing and the Chinese writing system. He is also said to have taught the earliest people life skills such as farming and animal husbandry.

L

Lao Zi 老子 (lǎo zǐ) - (Lao Tzu) The Chinese thinker and philosopher who is said to have scripted the Dao De Jing (see, Dao De Jing) at the request of a city gatekeeper when Lao Zi departed the city for the last time. Lao Zi was instrumental in establishing the "universe-view" in the Chinese cultural mindset.

M

Meridians 穴位 (xué wèi) - Also known as pressure points. Meridians are energy points that connect the flow of life energy throughout the body. In the idea of Chinese Traditional Medicine, optimal health is achieved when there is no congestion of the meridians and energy is allowed to flow freely.

Q

Qigong 气功 (qì gōng) - (Chi-Gong) A martial art practice based on the breath and universal energy flow. The character 气 (qì) means life energy and breath.

S

Skillful - This refers to an action or thought that is good or kind in nature. It is contrary to "unskillful." (See, unskillful)

Shaolin Kung Fu 少林功夫 (shǎo lín gōng fu) - A style of Kung Fu practiced by the monks at the Shaolin Temple. It is a stringent and mind-based form of Kung Fu.

Soft versus hard 柔弱胜刚强 (róu ruǎn shēng gāng qiáng) - A concept based on yin-yang, found in the Dao De Jing that supports the idea that soft energies and forces prevail hard. Consider the teeth (hard) and tongue (soft). Many lose their teeth but few lose the tongue.

T

Tai Chi 太极拳 (tài jí quán) - (Shadow Boxing) A slow-form Chinese Martial Art. Tai Chi is used for grounding the mind and the body while training slow-motion physical balance. There are several styles of Tai Chi, some longer and some shorter. The breath and mindfulness are also incorporated into the practice.

Taiji 太极 - The Chinese name for the yin-yang symbol, the black and white fish. It is a symbol that represents the two expressions of yin-yang (See, yin-yang), opposite, but not aggressive energies that create a whole.

The breath - (See, Breath)

U

Unskillful - This refers to an action or thought that is not good or kind in nature. It is contrary to "skillful." (See, skillful)

Y

Yin-yang 阴阳 (yín yáng) (pr. yeen-yahng) - Yin-yang is the concept authored in the Yi Jing (See, Yi Jing). Yin-yang are two expressions of one whole such as cool-warm, feminine-masculine, good-bad. Many of the 'wholes' may not be immediately apparent and there may not be a word to express them. All things can be arranged into yin-yang in some way. Two opposite but not aggressive forces or energies that make up a whole. I.e. Day, a whole, is formed by two opposites, daytime and night.

Yi Jing 易经 (yì jīng) - (I Ching or Book of Changes) A Chinese oracle of wisdom. The Yi Jing is a complex system of viewing the universe through the lens of yin-yang interactions. There are 64 hexagrams that make up the system. Each hexagram is made up of six components or levels, each of which is either yin or yang.

Made in the USA
Middletown, DE
20 March 2022

62678007R00068